modern
country cooking

TRADITIONAL RECIPES FOR CONTEMPORARY COOKS

Shona Crawford Poole

Photography by Peter Williams

COLLINS & BROWN

First published in the United Kingdom in 2005 by
Collins & Brown
151 Freston Road
London
W10 6TH

An imprint of Anova Books Company Ltd

This edition first published in 2007

ISBN-10: 1-84340-431-1
ISBN-13: 978-1-84340-431-6

A CIP catalogue record for this book is available from
the British Library.

10 9 8 7 6 5 4 3 2 1

Reproduction by Classicscan, Singapore
Printed and bound by Craft Print International Ltd,
Singapore

This book can be ordered direct from the publisher.
Contact the marketing department, but try your
bookshop first.

www.anovabooks.com

contents

Introduction   6

Dairy   8

Meat   30

Vegetables   54

Fish   76

Baking   96

Preserves   114

Desserts   126

Index   140

Useful Addresses   144

introduction

Country cooking is about wholesome freshness, good sense and tradition. It is cooking which has roots that connect it to local and seasonal produce, or to use the fashionable phrase, it has 'terroir'. So what is modern country cooking? All of the above, of course, and a bit more. Modern country cooking is for here and now in the twenty-first century.

Modernity can mean many different things. Sometimes 'modern' means a lighter, more refined or less calorific take on traditional dishes that evolved to satisfy appetites sharpened by heavy outdoor work and living in houses which had no central heating. Now we go a bit easier on suet puddings, frying in lard, double cream and melted cheese.

Sometimes 'modern' means less salty. It is not so long ago that we learned that too much salt is indisputably bad for human health. But that knowledge does not stop us craving the flavours of bacon, ham, smoked salmon, kippers and many more favourite foodstuffs that were once preserves. These no longer need the antibacterial protection provided by heavy salting at a time when there were no fridges and freezers; so modern salting is lighter. The same is true of foodstuffs that are heavily smoked or rely on sugar to preserve them.

Cooking has to adapt to take account of how ingredients change over the years. Today's hams, for example, are unlikely to need soaking before boiling, which is surely a change for the better. Other ingredients have also changed for the better. Easy-blend yeast for baking is simpler to store and even quicker to use than highly perishable fresh yeast, which is becoming increasingly hard to find.

If only change was always an improvement. There are times when 'modern' means finding good things to do with ingredients that have changed for the worse. Take the bulk of supermarket strawberries. They are now as crisp as apples, bred to travel well and look good, but too often a far cry from the sweetly perfumed, crushable berries of old.

Then there are ingredients that are not better or worse, only different. Many old recipes for chocolate-flavoured puddings and cakes need updating to take account of the superior quality of the chocolate that is now widely available. Better chocolate won't make a better mousse, only a heavier one if chocolate with a higher proportion of cocoa solids is substituted withouth adjusting the recipe. The flavour may be more intense, but a secondary consequence is akin to adding extra flour.

There are times when being 'modern' involves a flash of creative inspiration. Giving an old favourite a new twist that really works is as satisfying as cookery writing gets. Though I say so myself, curing fresh salmon with gin and juniper to make a variation on traditional dill-flavoured gravadlax illustrates just such a moment of inspiration.

All too often these days, politics and ethics intrude on our choice of ingredients, raising issues which are hard enough to keep abreast of, let alone to resolve. Planning a shopping list that considers sustainable agriculture, animal welfare, fair trade, food miles, dwindling fish stocks, genetic modification, organics, recyclable packaging, and the ever more extraordinary wonders of food technology, is a very contemporary and ultimately personal puzzle.

Modern country cooking is essentially home cooking at its contemporary best. It is about dishes that are better made at home than bought ready to eat or reheat. A fresh fruit tart, enjoyed on the day it is baked, will always be better than a factory-made tart in a box. The same is true, I hope, of all the recipes in this book – which is one reason why you won't find a conventional mix of dishes here. There is, for example, an extravagantly eggy recipe for fresh pasta, which is miles better than its packaged competitors. But you won't find a recipe for an eggless, hard wheat pasta because the finest dried pasta, good spaghetti for example, is factory-made. Nor will you find instructions for home-made butter puff pastry because that, in another change for the better, can now be bought ready-made too. No one says home cooks, even the best of them, always make the best of everything.

Another reason for this eclectic selection of recipes is that they have all been published on the cookery pages of *Country Living* Magazine over the past few years. So while there are recipes for every season, you won't find dishes for all the most commonly available ingredients, or for every conceivable occasion.

Lastly, and firstly too, there is the dream of living at a pace civilized enough to bake your own bread, cultivate a garden, harvest the fruit and fill the kitchen with the heavenly smells of baking and jam-making. It is a timeless rural idyll. Modern country cooking is about keeping that tradition alive, too.

dairy

Country cooks have always enjoyed the freshest eggs and milk, the richest cream and the creamiest new butter. In recent years, the choice of locally produced foods has expanded with the renaissance of artisan dairying and cheesemaking. Fresh cheeses based on the milk of goats, sheep and water buffalo have joined the ranks of new and traditional cow's milk cheeses at farmers' markets and on cheese counters. It is no bad thing to be so spoiled for choice that it is as easy to find milky-sweet fresh ricotta as it is to settle for blandly boring cottage cheese.

Many of us like to decorate our kitchens with dairy collectables, such as pierced pottery cheese-drainers, shallow cream bowls and skimmers, or wooden blocks delicately carved in intaglio for impressing patterns on butter. Many of these patterns tell a story. Usually, they identify the type of farm on which the butter was made – a swan for a farm with water meadow grazing, a sprig of bog myrtle for a hill firm, or a cow to celebrate a prizewinning beast.

Butter, much like oysters, was once an important food of the poor as well as of princes. In spring and summer, when grazing was lush and milk was rich and plentiful, country people made their own butter. Many families kept a cow, ate butter with bread and herbs while it was fresh and sweet, then salted down the surplus for winter. Often it was so heavily salted that it had to be washed with spring water before it was fit to eat.

We seem to have lost the idea that butter is a preserve, and that it evolved as a way of extending the useful life of milk, just as cheese does. Butter is simply the fat in cream, gathered up and separated from the liquid part of the milk by churning.

For a time, dairy produce (especially butter, cream, full-fat cheese and egg yolks) got a bad press on health grounds, over concerns about the role of its saturated fats in raising cholesterol levels. More recent research offers new hope to food-lovers. Moderation, not elimination, is advised. Sales of butter have risen again, along with its status. It has been transformed from an unremarkable necessity to an indulgence and a luxury, for there is no denying that nearly everyone prefers the taste of butter to any of its many imitators. Indeed, some dishes are simply unthinkable without the flavour of best butter. On my list are tender spears of home-grown green asparagus dipped in melted butter, and buttery toast soldiers to dunk in soft-boiled eggs.

Simplicity is the hallmark of the all the best-loved egg dishes. An omelette, softly scrambled or lightly poached eggs on toast, or fried eggs and bacon can be rustled up in minutes and cooked as quickly for one as for half a dozen. All rely on high-quality eggs, which will certainly be free-range and very likely organic.

The obstacles that newly laid eggs place in the path of the cook – for example the near impossibility of peeling a hard-boiled, very fresh egg without taking off much of the white with the shell, or of whisking the raw whites to a respectable meringue – are problems that most of us would be lucky to encounter. Except, perhaps, by buying at the farm gate or a farmers' market, the freshest eggs on sale are invariably several days old. Even when stored in ideal conditions, eggs deteriorate from the moment they are laid. They lose moisture through their porous shells; the whites gradually become thinner and the yolks more fragile. These are just the changes we can see. Older eggs are less efficient raisers of cakes, setters of custards, and emulsifiers of sauces. So it makes sense to buy the freshest eggs you can find and to use them as soon as possible. As for storage, unless you have a cool larder (10°C and not too dry is optimum), the refrigerator is the best place.

For the cook, an egg is a beautifully packaged chemistry set. Whisk air into the whites and the resultant foam can be used to to raise soufflés and cakes, to lighten batters, or sweetened and dried to a crisp to make meringues. The yolks will thicken and set custards and fruit curds, bind pastry and glaze pies, and, most magical of all, hold together those dangerous liaisons, the classic emulsion

sauces: hollandaise, béarnaise and mayonnaise. If any recipes deserve to be thought of as magic formulas, as spells for transforming base ingredients into gold, these sauces top the list. And as befits spells, they involve an element of risk, for emulsions are reputed to be tricky and temperamental to make, prone to split and curdle at a moment's inattention. But nothing you can buy in a jar comes anywhere near the silky richness of a freshly home-made emulsion, and making it unhurriedly by hand is a pleasure in itself. It is all a matter of starting slowly and working steadily. Think of it as a therapeutic activity and double the pleasure – first making, then eating.

creamed eggs
with caviar

For a very special breakfast, or a casual first course, creamed eggs topped with caviar are fun and festive. More affordable toppings, which taste equally good, include slivers of smoked salmon or smoked eel, or golden salmon eggs that burst on the tongue. Serves four.

8 very fresh eggs

2 teaspoons butter, softened

salt and freshly ground black pepper

1 tablespoon double cream

50g shallots, very finely chopped

½ tablespoon finely chopped chives

60–100g caviar

TO SERVE
12 soldiers of crustless toasted bread

Slice the tops off the eggs at the wider end. Empty six of the eggs into one bowl and two (to be used for another recipe) into another.

Wash and dry all eight eggshells and 'hats'.

Lightly whisk the six eggs and strain them.

Melt the butter in a small pan over a low heat and add the beaten eggs. Cook over a gentle heat, slowly increasing the temperature and whisking continuously. Keep the temperature under 65°C, whisking until the eggs form a light, creamy mass. This takes about 10 unhurried minutes.

Remove the pan from the heat and season the eggs with salt and pepper. Whisk in the cream, raw shallots and chives.

Set the eggshells in eggcups and divide the creamed eggs between them. Top each filled egg with a teaspoonful of caviar, and arrange its eggshell hat at a jaunty angle. Serve warm with toast soldiers.

Creamed eggs are equally good served cold, in which case add the fishy topping after the eggs have cooled completely.

baked eggs
with cream & chives

When a dish is as simple and timeless as this, the quality of the eggs is paramount. Chives give an instant gentle onion flavour to a dish, without the need for cooking. Take a sharp knife or scissors to a bundle of really fresh chives and the crisp feel is like cutting silk taffeta. Serves six.

15g butter

6 very fresh eggs

8 tablespoons pourable double cream

2 tablespoons finely chopped chives

salt and cayenne pepper

TO SERVE
toast

Heat the oven to 200°C/180°C fan oven/gas mark 6.

Use half the butter to grease six small ovenproof dishes or ramekins. Break an egg into each dish. Mix the cream with the chives and season it rather highly with salt and pepper, as this will be seasoning the egg too. Divide the cream between the eggs.

Stand the dishes in a roasting tin and pour in boiling water to come halfway up their sides. Bake for about 7 minutes for eggs with just-set whites and soft yolks, longer if the eggs are straight from the fridge, or if you prefer set yolks.

Eat at once with toast.

Variations: finely chopped fresh tarragon, chervil and parsley work well with eggs, singly or mixed, and with or without the oniony whiff of chives.

bacon & egg salad

Warm salads mix spring freshness and winter comfort with just the right between-seasons touch. They are a tonic to the taste buds, too. Poach the eggs in advance, and multiplying the number of servings is as easy as pie. Serves two.

½ a ficelle, the thinnest French stick loaf

1 tablespoon olive oil

about 100g mixed leaves, including dandelion and curly endive

100g dry-cured, smoked streaky bacon in one piece

2 tablespoons red wine vinegar

salt and freshly ground black pepper

2 eggs, lightly poached *

Warm the plates. Slice the bread thinly on the diagonal. Brush or spray the slices of bread with olive oil and grill them until golden on both sides. Keep warm. Put the leaves in a large bowl.

Remove the bacon rind (if any) and cut the bacon into thick matchsticks. Cook in a heavy frying pan until the fat has run out and the bacon is crisp. Remove and keep warm.

Pour off all but a tablespoonful of the bacon fat and add the vinegar, plus a couple of tablespoonfuls of water to the pan. Scrape the bacon brownings into the liquid, let it reduce a little and season with freshly ground black pepper. Taste before adding any salt: it may not need it.

Pour this dressing over the salad and mix well. Divide the leaves between the warm plates, add the croutons and bacon lardons, and top with poached eggs (see below). Eat while the dressing and egg are still warm.

* The poached egg trick

Perfect poached eggs can be cooked in advance and reheated. Here's how. You will need the freshest possible eggs and a wide, shallow pan with a lid. In it, bring a finger's depth of water to the boil. Do not add salt or vinegar. Turn off the heat and add the eggs quickly, breaking them directly into the water and as near to its surface as possible. This helps to stop the whites spreading. Cover and leave undisturbed for 4 minutes. Don't cook more than four at once, or the water will lose too much heat and the eggs will be difficult to lift out without breaking them.

Using a perforated slice, lift the eggs on to a clean, damp cloth, trim away the raggedy edges and submerge them in cold water. They can now be chilled and kept for up to 24 hours.

To reheat and serve, lift the eggs into another shallow dish and pour in boiling water to cover them. They will be ready in just 1 minute.

cheese pudding

This is a sort of savoury bread and butter pudding with an almost soufflé-like texture and thin golden crust. It is a comforting, homely dish that makes thrifty good use of odds and ends of good bread and strong cheese. Serves two to three.

3 eggs

2 teaspoons Dijon mustard

500ml full-cream milk

100g white breadcrumbs from a loaf a day or more old

120g strong, hard cheese, grated

salt and freshly ground black pepper

chives (optional), finely snipped

TO SERVE
mixed green leaf salad

Break the eggs into a bowl, add the mustard and whisk lightly. Stir in the milk, breadcrumbs, cheese, seasonings and chives. If you have time, set the mixture aside for half an hour or more to allow the breadcrumbs to soak up the liquid.

Stir to redistribute the ingredients and pour into a well-buttered 1-litre oven dish. Set the filled dish in another, larger one, and place on the middle shelf of an oven preheated to 180°C/160°C fan oven/gas mark 4. Half-fill the outer dish with boiling water and bake for about 45 minutes or until set, well risen and golden.

Serve hot, with a mixed green leaf salad.

broad bean omelette
with mint & ricotta

Broad beans, the smaller and younger the better, are one of the first summer vegetables; but no matter how young, the beans are nicer peeled. Celebrate the arrival of broad beans and new shoots of mint in this lovely omelette. It is a complete meal on its own. Serves one.

2 or 3 eggs

2 tablespoons broad beans, blanched and peeled

2 teaspoons chopped chives

1 teaspoon chopped mint

salt and freshly ground black pepper

1 teaspoon butter

2 tablespoons fresh ricotta cheese

Break the eggs into a bowl and whisk them together lightly. Add the beans, chives, mint and a generous seasoning of salt and freshly ground black pepper. Mix.

Heat a heavy omelette pan and add the butter. If the butter foams immediately, without browning, the heat is perfect. (If the butter browns immediately, the pan is too hot. Let it cool a little, wipe it out and start again.) Tip in the egg mixture.

Draw the setting egg at the sides of the pan towards the centre, letting the uncooked egg run to the edges. When the egg is almost set, dot the omelette with small blobs of ricotta. Roll the omelette on to a warmed plate and eat with fresh, crusty bread.

pastry cream

This is the stuff of custard slices, and the unctuous layer in raspberry or strawberry tarts between crisp, sweet pastry and fresh berries. It is a very easy custard to make, because it is stabilized with a little flour, which prevents the egg from curdling. Makes about 500ml.

450ml full-cream milk

Put the milk and vanilla pod in a small pan, bring to the boil, remove from the heat and leave to infuse, ideally until cold.

1 vanilla pod, split lengthways

5 egg yolks

Combine the egg yolks, sugar and salt in a bowl and whisk until pale and dense. Add the flour and cornflour and whisk again. Strain the milk and add it gradually to the egg mixture, whisking well. Rinse and dry the vanilla pod and use it to perfume a jar of sugar.

100g vanilla sugar or caster sugar

a pinch of salt

Pour the mixture back into the pan. Bring to the boil on a moderate heat, stirring constantly. There is an alarming moment when the custard looks like scrambled egg. Take courage, keep beating until it is smooth, and cook for 3 minutes more.

2 tablespoons plain flour

1 tablespoon cornflour

Remove the pan from the heat and beat in the butter. Beat for a little longer until the custard begins to cool, then cover and chill it. Stir in the liqueur, if you are using it, when the custard is cold.

15g unsalted butter

1 tablespoon Benedictine (optional)

a custard made with cream

Make this with cream and no flour to layer in trifles (page 132).

6 egg yolks

Whisk the egg yolks until they are pale and fluffy.

600ml double cream

Bring the cream to the boil in a saucepan and pour it over the egg yolks, whisking continuously. Return the custard to the pan and cook it very gently without allowing it to boil, stirring constantly until it thickens.

about 50g caster sugar

vanilla extract to taste

Take it off the heat and stir in the sugar and vanilla extract to taste, allowing for cooling to diminish the flavour a little. Use hot or cover and cool.

fresh egg pasta

There is a liveliness about freshly home-made egg pasta, which cannot be matched by the so-called fresh pasta sold in packets. Long use-by dates and freshness make incompatible bedfellows.

This extravagantly eggy pasta is no empty carb fest. Use it with your own fillings to make the best ravioli you will ever eat, or to make plain tagliatelle to eat with butter and cheese. Alternatively, make silk handkerchiefs, mandilli de soea, by rolling the dough as thinly as possible, and cutting it into 10cm squares. Cook these in the usual way and serve with freshly made pesto. Makes 1kg.

250g flour

250g fine semolina

400g egg yolks (about 16–20 egg yolks)

2 whole eggs

Mix the flour and semolina and combine with the egg yolks and whole eggs to make a stiff dough. Knead the dough very thoroughly, cover it in clingfilm and chill for an hour before rolling out.

Divide the dough into eight pieces and cover seven. Flatten one ball, dust it with flour and roll it into a long, wide strip, starting at the coarsest roller setting of the pasta machine and working down to the finest for ravioli or mandilli de soea. For tagliatelle, stop at the second-finest setting, then run the rolled strips through the cutting blades. Repeat for the other seven pieces.

pumpkin ravioli
with sage & parmesan

Pumpkin ravioli is an Italian classic, and quite the best thing made with pumpkin that I have ever eaten. Serve it with butter and fried sage leaves. Serves six to eight.

FOR THE PUMPKIN FILLING
1kg butternut squash or pumpkin, in 2 or 3 pieces

400g fresh ricotta cheese, well drained

200g finely grated Parmesan cheese

2 amaretti biscuits, crumbled

salt and freshly ground black pepper

freshly grated nutmeg

TO ASSEMBLE
1 batch fresh egg pasta dough (page 20)

flour and fine semolina for rolling

1 beaten egg

TO COOK AND SERVE
100g butter

12 or more fresh sage leaves

freshly ground black pepper

6 tablespoons finely grated Parmesan

Heat the oven to 160°C/140°C fan oven/gas mark 3. Bake the squash or pumpkin for about 1½ hours. When the flesh is very soft, discard the skin and seeds and turn the flesh into a wide pan. Slowly cook off the moisture without letting the purée stick or burn, reducing the volume by about half.

Combine the reduced purée with the ricotta, Parmesan and Amaretti crumbs, and season well with salt, black pepper and nutmeg.

Divide the dough into four pieces and cover three. Flatten one ball, dust it with flour and roll it into a long, wide strip, starting at the coarsest roller setting of the pasta machine and working down to the finest. Place the first strip of dough on a lightly floured surface. Dot small balls of stuffing at intervals along one edge of the strip. Paint beaten egg between the balls of stuffing and along the edge. Fold over the pasta to cover the stuffing. Press to seal between the balls of stuffing, then seal the open edge. Cut out the ravioli, check the sealed edges, dredge in semolina and arrange in a single layer on a tray that has been liberally dusted with semolina.

Roll and fill the remaining dough in the same way. However dry your stuffing, and it should be as dry as possible, never stack ravioli on top of each other or they will stick and tear.

To cook and serve the ravioli, allow at least six pieces per serving and cook no more than six servings at a time. Bring a big pan of salted water to the boil. In a large, shallow pan, gently melt the butter with the sage and pepper.

Drop the ravioli into the boiling water and cook for 4 minutes after the water has come back to a gentle boil. Test whether they are done with your teeth, and cook a little longer if needed. Use a wide, flat draining ladle to transfer the ravioli to the pan of melted sage butter. Turn up the heat and carefully turn the ravioli in the butter, then serve at once with the buttery juices, sage leaves and a sprinkling of Parmesan.

basil & ricotta ravioli

Fresh ricotta has a lovely sweet, milky flavour. Make the ravioli as described on page 20, using the ingredients below for the filling. Boil it in the usual way, then serve with a knob of butter to melt on the pasta, and a sprinkling of Parmesan. Or go one better and serve the ravioli floating in well-flavoured chicken stock anointed with a few drops of truffle oil. Serves six.

FOR THE FILLING
500g very fresh ricotta cheese, well drained

6 tablespoons finely chopped basil

4 tablespoons finely chopped chives

4 tablespoons finely chopped flat-leaved parsley

4 tablespoons finely grated Parmesan

salt and freshly ground black pepper

freshly grated nutmeg

TO ASSEMBLE
1 batch fresh egg pasta dough (page 20)

flour and fine semolina for rolling

1 beaten egg

TO COOK AND SERVE
100g butter, diced

6 tablespoons finely grated Parmesan

Combine all the filling ingredients in a bowl and mix together. Season the mixture well to counteract the blandness of the pasta dough.

Divide the dough into four pieces and cover three. Flatten one ball, dust it with flour and roll it into a long, wide strip, starting at the coarsest roller setting of the pasta machine and working down to the finest. Place the first strip of dough on a lightly floured surface. Put small balls of stuffing at intervals along one edge of the strip. Paint beaten egg between the balls of stuffing and along the edge. Fold over the pasta to cover the stuffing. Press to seal between the balls of stuffing, then seal the open edge. Cut out the ravioli, check the sealed edges, dredge in semolina and arrange in a single layer on a tray that has been liberally dusted with semolina.

Roll and fill the remaining dough in the same way. However dry the stuffing, and it should be as dry as possible, never stack ravioli on top of each other or they will stick and tear.

To cook and serve the ravioli, allow at least six pieces per serving and cook no more than six servings at a time. Bring a big pan of salted water to the boil. Drop the ravioli into the boiling water and cook for 4 minutes after the water has come back to a gentle boil. Test whether they are done with your teeth, and cook a little longer if needed.

Drain the ravioli and return them to the pan with the diced butter, half the grated Parmesan and some more black pepper. Toss lightly together and serve at once on heated plates, handing round the rest of the Parmesan.

herb butter

A pat of butter flavoured with herbs, melting over meat, poultry or fish sizzling from the grill or barbecue, is the simplest of sauces. It offsets the drying effects of grilling and adds a lift of flavour. Don't be afraid to experiment with new tastes: see Variations. Makes 250g.

250g unsalted butter, softened

2 tablespoons fresh lemon juice

4 tablespoons finely chopped parsley

2 tablespoons finely chopped chives

2 tablespoons finely chopped chervil

salt

freshly ground black pepper or cayenne pepper

In a bowl, cream the butter. Beat in the lemon juice, herbs and a little salt and pepper or cayenne pepper. Taste and adjust the seasoning, remembering that the finished butter is intended to add flavour.

Shape the butter into a roll and cover it with greaseproof paper, or clingfilm. Chill well.

Just before serving, cut the chilled butter into pats. Melt them over freshly grilled or barbecued meat, poultry or fish.

Variations

For white fish, try an aniseed-flavoured French aperitif such as Pernod to make flavoured butter – about 1 tablespoonful per 100g of butter.

The sharp, sour flavours of citrus work well with fish too – mix the juice of Seville orange, lime or lemon, perhaps with a little of the finely grated zest, with the butter.

Tarragon and chervil butter, made with a splash of lemon juice, does good things for chicken.

Tinned or bottled green peppercorns, mashed and mixed with butter, dress steaks and give boring burgers a hit of heat.

hollandaise sauce

Buttery, eggy hollandaise is simply the finest sauce yet devised for asparagus, globe artichokes, or for a handsome piece of poached halibut or turbot. Although it is best made and served without delay, the sauce can be kept warm for a short period at 50°C if you have reliable temperature control. Overheating risks curdling the sauce. Makes about 300ml.

250g unsalted butter, softened

1 tablespoon fresh lemon juice, strained

sea salt and pepper

4 egg yolks

cold water, as needed

To make the sauce by hand, cut the butter into cubes. Mix the lemon juice and ½ teaspoonful each of salt and pepper in the top of a double boiler, or in a bowl set over a pan of hot water. The water in the base should barely simmer and be kept below boiling point throughout.

Add the egg yolks to the pan and whisk briskly until the mixture becomes pale and thick.

Add the butter, a couple of cubes at a time, incorporating each batch very thoroughly before adding the next. Controlling the heat is key – too hot and it will curdle, too little heat and the sauce will take an age to thicken.

You can lighten the sauce with cold water (2 or 3 tablespoonfuls) incorporated at the end. For a particularly thick and glossy hollandaise more suitable for fish than for vegetables, make it with clarified butter (page 28).

To make the sauce in a food processor or blender, first warm the goblet in hot water and heat the butter to boiling, but do not allow it to brown. Put the lemon juice, salt, pepper and egg yolks into the warmed goblet and process them until thick. Add the melted butter, starting slowly and gradually increasing the stream as the sauce thickens. To finish, check the seasoning, adding more salt, pepper or lemon juice to taste.

mayonnaise

Summer without a bowl of shining, wobbling mayonnaise to partner cold salmon is all but unthinkable. Home-made mayonnaise dresses the best potato salads and reinvents coleslaw. Good olive oil does not necessarily make good mayonnaise. Avoid anything too pugnaciously flavoured, or use a little to flavour a sauce based on a blander, lighter oil such as sunflower or groundnut. Makes about 500ml.

3 egg yolks

sea salt and pepper

500ml lightly flavoured oil

1 tablespoon wine or cider vinegar or lemon juice

To make mayonnaise by hand, put the egg yolks in a bowl, add ¼ teaspoonful salt and a little pepper and whisk until smooth and beginning to thicken.

Now start adding the oil, a teaspoonful at a time, whisking constantly. Make sure each addition of oil is thoroughly incorporated before adding the next. Once the mixture begins to keep its shape, the oil can be added in a slow and steady stream as long as the beating is equally continuous.

When about half the oil has been incorporated, beat in half the vinegar or lemon juice, then continue slowly adding the rest of the oil and beating.

Finally, stir in the remaining vinegar or lemon juice to taste and adjust the seasoning if necessary.

To make mayonnaise in a food processor or blender, put the yolks, seasonings and all the vinegar or lemon juice into the goblet and blend well before beginning to add the oil in a steady stream, keeping the machine running, until all the oil has been incorporated. You may need to add two or more tablespoonfuls of water at intervals to stop the mayonnaise thickening too much and splitting.

potted crab

If crab sandwiches are summer seaside fare, potted crab on hot toast is a fireside treat. You can use a mixture of white and brown crabmeat, or white meat only. Serves six.

400g very fresh crabmeat

Pick over the crabmeat to make sure there are no shell fragments in it.

150g unsalted butter

Warm the butter just enough to melt it and stir in the crabmeat, mace, cayenne and a little salt. Taste and adjust the seasoning.

about ½ teaspoon ground mace

about ¼ teaspoon cayenne pepper

Pack the mixture into a single dish, or divide it equally between six small pots or ramekins. Cover and chill until firm.

salt

Heat the clarified butter just enough to melt it, and pour it over the surface of the potted crab to seal it. The amount of butter needed will depend on the size and number of the pots. Top with a bay leaf, cover and chill.

about 100g clarified butter

6 small bay leaves

Give potted crab at least 24 hours in the refrigerator to allow the flavours to mingle and develop. Serve with hot, thick toast.

clarified butter

Clarified butter is pure butter fat that has been cleansed of butter's residual milk proteins and liquid. It is valuable for frying, when it can be heated to high temperatures without burning. It is the traditional sealing layer on potted crab and shrimp, which reminds us that this is a time-honoured method of short-term preservation from the days before refrigeration. Makes about 400g.

500g unsalted butter

Melt the butter in a heavy pan on a low heat. Bring it to the gentlest of simmers and hold it at this temperature, without stirring, until all the sediment has fallen to the bottom of the pan and the liquid butter is clear. This will take 30 minutes or more.

Line a fine sieve with a double layer of muslin or cheesecloth and strain the liquid butter into a bowl or jar, leaving the sediment in the pan. Allow the butter to cool completely before covering it and storing in a cool place.

meat

In terms of quality, meat is the most variable of the raw materials
we cook. If you know where to look for good meat, it has never
been better. Thanks to the passion of farmers who have resisted
agro-business demands for fast-growing, unnaturally lean beasts, and
to the work of the Rare Breeds Survival Trust, the choice of meat we
can buy is wider than ever.

Locally produced meat that I have gone back to farmers' markets to
buy repeatedly include Sussex beef from cattle grazed on the South
Downs, pork from Tamworth, Gloucester Old Spot and Middle
White pigs, and partridge, pheasant, pigeon and venison from local
shoots. Overnight couriers have brought deliveries of Welsh lamb
from Snowdonia and the Anglesey salt marshes, Herdwick lamb
from Cumbria, organic ducks and geese from Exmoor, wild boar
from Scotland, pork from Devon, and chicken livers from birds
reared organically in Berkshire. All these, which are only a small
selection from the wide choice of meat and poultry available directly
from the producers, have been well worth repeat orders.

Rare breed pork has been a revelation. I had all but given up cooking pork because it was being bred too lean to have good flavour or succulence. Now pork is back on the menu and as a bonus, breeds of pig that were heading for extinction are thriving again due to the revival of demand for their excellent meat. The same holds true for rare breed sheep, cattle and poultry.

Most meat that is worth eating has some visible fat on it – game being the flavoursome exception. This is a fact that nutritional propaganda about avoiding saturated fats cannot change. The best answer to reducing the amount of saturated fat we eat cannot be to breed animals with meat so lean that its flavour, texture and cooking qualities are ruined. Surely it is better to eat great-tasting meat less frequently, rather than mediocre meat daily. Industrially farmed meat, at its worst, is not worth eating. The meat of an intensively reared chicken that has reached premature maturity de-beaked and routinely medicated, without access to daylight or space to behave naturally, is the tasteless pap that gets chicken a bad name and should give everyone a bad conscience. And that's before it is subjected to food processing to bulk up the flesh with water and chemicals.

Top-quality chicken meat comes from slower-growing breeds reared in conditions that allow them to thrive without routine mutilation and routine antibiotics. Buying organically certified birds is one way to ensure that the meat on your plate meets decent gastronomic and ethical standards. But of course it is not the only way. Quiz producers face to face at farmers' markets, talk to your local butcher, and read supermarket labels carefully.

Noting what shoppers are buying directly from specialist producers, the supermarkets are responding with premium ranges of their own. Individual farms and farmers star on labels for outdoor-reared pork, named breed and longer-hung beef, and some pretty fancy chickens. Behind the marketing hype, huge attention is paid to good husbandry and animal welfare not only because an increasing number of consumers are demonstrating with their purses that they care about animals being humanely treated, but because birds and animals make better meat when they lead healthy lives and meet a stress-free death. An unexpected spin-off of the success of organic produce is the way that the development of cutting-edge organic farming methods is helping to raise standards in conventional farming.

There are recipes in this chapter for salt beef, salt duck and confit of duck. Although salting was originally a method of preserving meat – as in bacon, smoked salmon and kippers – it is no longer a necessity when freezers make our food all but immortal. Any brining we do now is designed to produce particular tastes and textures that we have learned to relish. We know, of course, to be cautious about the quantity of salt we eat, but there is no need to banish these traditional dishes. Most of the salt used in the initial curing is washed off and cooked out, with the result that the end product is not salty, but perfectly seasoned.

These recipes for cured meats take time to prepare. So do a couple of other magnificent dishes in this chapter. Game is one of the glories of country cooking and I look forward, every year, to autumn and winter for roasts and casseroles of pheasant, partridge, wild duck and venison to name only the most readily available. Savour the appreciative murmuring that ripples around the table when a steamed partridge pudding is opened and its richly savoury smell swirls over the assembled company, and don't miss the looks of greedy anticipation that attend the knife poised to cut the crisp, golden edifice of a venison pasty raised, as tradition dictates, in hot-water crust pastry.

confit of duck legs

The legs of ducks and geese have less fat on them than the breast meat and even more flavour, and are often sold separately. This is the time to make confit, salting the meat lightly to draw off some of the moisture, then cooking it very slowly in its own fat until, as the old French recipes say, the meat can be pierced with a straw. Traditionally, confit is stored in its own cooking fat, but it is easier to use for an instant meal or in a cassoulet if it is kept in the refrigerator or freezer. Serves six.

6 duck legs or 4 goose legs (about 1.2kg)

30g sea salt

2 bay leaves

2 sprigs thyme

½ teaspoon black peppercorns

about 1 litre/1kg tinned goose fat, or fresh duck or goose fat

TO SERVE
sautéd potatoes

green salad

Using a pestle and mortar, grind together the salt, bay leaves, thyme and peppercorns. Rub this mixture into the legs and pack them into a dish. Cover and refrigerate for 12 to 14 hours.

Heat the oven to 140°C/120°C fan oven/gas mark 1. Choose an ovenproof casserole that will hold all the legs snugly, and melt the duck or goose fat in it. Dry the salted legs and rub off any visible salt. Pack them into the casserole and cook them for 2 hours, or until meltingly tender.

Carefully lift the legs from the cooking fat and put them (in one layer) in a covered dish. Chill or freeze until needed.

To heat the confit put it on a tray in a moderately hot oven (200°C/180°C fan oven/gas mark 6) for 25–30 minutes; or heat it slowly in a frying pan, raising the heat at the end to crisp the skin. Serve with potatoes sautéed in a little of the goose fat and a green salad with a sharpish sweet-sour dressing.

salt duck

Eaten cold, duck that has been salted and then poached in stock is a real treat. It goes without saying that the starting point is a decent duck, the larger the better. Serves four as a main course.

1 duck, 2kg or more

150g sea salt

500ml giblet stock

Rub the duck with the salt inside and out and set it in a covered dish in the refrigerator. Turn the duck, morning and night, for three days.

Heat the oven to 150°C/130°C fan oven/gas mark 2. Rinse the duck thoroughly in cold water and set it in a casserole. In a pan, bring the stock to the boil and pour it over the duck. Cover the casserole and cook in the oven for two hours, or until the bird is tender. Let it cool in its stock. Skin the duck before carving the velvety meat.

salt brisket

Allow seven to ten days for salting the meat. Once salted, it will keep in the refrigerator for a few days, or it can be frozen. In an ideal world, you would have a capacious lidded crock to hold the brine, but a plastic bucket or box will do nicely. Salt beef is good hot or cold, so it is well worth curing a sizeable chunk. Makes about ten servings.

2.5kg to 3kg boned brisket of beef in one piece

200g sea salt

½ teaspoon saltpetre (optional)

100g light muscovado sugar

1 teaspoon black peppercorns

First check that the crock or bucket is spotlessly clean. Have ready a clean plate to hold the meat down in the brine, and a suitable weight to keep it submerged (a metal weight encased in a plastic bag, or a filled glass jar).

If the brisket has been rolled, cut the strings and lay it out flat. Crush together the salt, saltpetre if you are using it, sugar and peppercorns. Rub the mixture into the meat on all sides. Put the meat in the crock or bucket and cover it with cold water. Put a plate on top of the meat and sink it with the weight. Cover to keep out dust and insects and stand in a cool place for seven to ten days. Turn the meat in the pickle every couple of days.

Don't worry if the brine becomes a bit slippery – as long as it smells wholesome, it is fine. See page 38 for cooking instructions.

boiled beef
& dumplings

A fine piece of brisket, salted (see page 37) and cooked at home with fluffy dumplings and plainly boiled vegetables, makes a feast to remember. Serves six, with leftovers of meat to eat cold.

2.5kg to 3kg piece of salt brisket

14 medium carrots, scraped

14 medium onions, peeled

large sprig of thyme

2 bay leaves

6 small white turnips, or scraped parsnips

FOR THE DUMPLINGS
250g self-raising flour

½ teaspoon salt

½ teaspoon freshly ground black pepper

125g shredded suet

4 tablespoons finely chopped parsley

TO SERVE
boiled potatoes

freshly made English mustard, or horseradish

Rinse the salt brisket in cold water, then roll and tie it tightly. Put it in a large pan and cover it with fresh cold water. Bring slowly to the boil. Immediately reduce the heat, skim well and add 2 of the carrots, 2 onions, and the thyme and bay. Cover and simmer very gently until tender, about 4 hours in total.

About 40 minutes before the beef is ready, fish out the flavouring vegetables which will be mushy, and add the remaining carrots and onions, and the turnips or parsnips.

Sift the flour, salt and pepper into a bowl, add the suet and chopped parsley and toss gently together. Gradually add enough cold water to form a soft dough. Divide the dough into 12 pieces and, using floured hands, shape them into balls. Chill the dumplings for 30 minutes.

There probably won't be enough room in the pot to cook the dumplings as well, so they are best cooked separately in some of the beef cooking liquor, or in boiling salted water.

Drop the dumplings into boiling stock or water, then cover and simmer for 20 minutes. If the water is boiling too briskly, they may disintegrate. If it is not hot enough, they will be leaden. Cooking them in a pan with a glass lid allows you to see what is happening. You can improvise by covering the pan with a glass plate or casserole lid.

Remove the beef from the pan and transfer it to a big, hot serving platter. Surround it with the drained vegetables. Add the dumplings. Strain and skim the cooking liquor and serve it in a heated jug. Fiery English mustard or horseradish cream and a dish of boiled potatoes complete the feast.

chicken
with rosemary & pine nuts

Rosemary, garlic and a hint of thyme combine to evoke the sunshine of Provence in this quickly assembled chicken bake, which could well become a family standby. Allow two or three chicken thighs per person, ideally from chickens that bring real flavour of their own to the dish. Serve with small potatoes baked or boiled in their skins or, almost divinely, a creamy potato gratin. Serves four to six.

12 chicken thighs

2 tablespoons fruity olive oil

2 cloves garlic, peeled

salt and freshly ground black pepper

4 sprigs rosemary

2 sprigs thyme

3 tablespoons pine nuts

Heat the oven to 220°C/200°C fan oven/gas mark 7. Choose a shallow baking dish that will hold the chicken pieces, not too snugly, in a single layer. Spread half the oil over the bottom of the dish. Crush the garlic cloves with a little salt, using the tip of a knife blade to mash them to a pulp. Rub the garlic into the chicken pieces and lay them in the dish, scattering rosemary needles, thyme leaves and seasoning under, over and between them. Sprinkle the remaining oil over the chicken and bake for about 35 minutes, basting once or twice.

Scatter the pine nuts over the chicken, baste it again and bake for another 10 to 15 minutes, or until the meat is cooked, the skin is golden and beginning to crisp, and the pine nuts are lightly coloured. Exact timing will depend on the size of the chicken pieces. Serve straight from the dish.

partridge pudding

A big, comforting pudding brimming with tender pieces of partridge in thick gravy is as good as a traditional suet pudding gets. It needs long, gentle and more or less unattended cooking, so it fits in beautifully with the family walks and afternoon naps that the festive season demands. I start one, or even two days in advance. Cut off the legs and breast meat and put these in the fridge. Use the carcasses, plus a couple of chopped onions, carrots and celery sticks, to make stock. As this needs to be cold when assembling the pudding, it pays to get ahead. Serves six to eight.

6 to 8 partridge, meat removed and carcasses used for stock

2 tablespoons plain flour well seasoned with salt and cayenne pepper

1 tablespoon finely chopped parsley

2 sprigs thyme

750ml partridge stock

FOR THE SUET CRUST
400g self-raising flour

100g fresh, fine white breadcrumbs

250g shredded suet

1½ teaspoons salt

iced water to mix

butter for the bowl

Choose a pudding basin that holds 2 litres (with room to spare) and a pan or casserole pot with a lid that is large enough to hold the filled bowl when it is standing on a trivet. To keep the pudding basin off the direct heat, put a trivet in the bottom, set the basin on it, and fill with water to come halfway up the basin. Take out and dry the basin, and put the water on the stove to heat. It needs to be on the boil when you have constructed the pudding.

Also, before you start, sort out some greaseproof paper and foil to cover the pudding basin, scissors, string and a big napkin or clean tea towel. Butter the inside of the bowl lavishly and set it aside.

Keep the partridge legs whole and divide each breast into two pieces. Put all the meat in a bag with the seasoned flour and shake well together. Add the herbs and shake again. Set aside.

To make the suet crust, combine the flour, breadcrumbs, suet and salt in a large bowl and mix thoroughly. Add iced water, a tablespoonful at a time, mixing lightly until the mixture makes a softish dough. Use your hands to bring it together at the end and press it lightly into a cohesive mass. Pull off about a quarter of the dough and set it aside to make a lid.

On a generously floured board, roll out the larger piece of dough into a circle to line the pudding basin. Fold it into four and drop it into the buttered basin, opening it out to mould against the sides, and leaving the excess draped over the sides. Don't worry if you are not very dextrous: any holes can be patched with offcuts pasted into place with a dab of water.

Give the filling a final shake in its bag, then fill the pudding basin with the floured pieces of partridge, starting with the breast meat and arranging the legs in a neat circle on top.

Pour in the cold stock to within 1cm of the top of the meat. Roll out the pastry for the top, using a plate or pan lid as a guide to make a circle that fits just inside the bowl. Lay the pastry lid on the meat. Trim the dough to leave an overhang of about 1cm. Brush the edge with water and fold the margin of pastry above the filling down over the lid and press lightly to seal.

Cover the bowl with the greaseproof paper and foil, tying it on tightly under the rim. Trim the papers back to 1cm or less. Lay a big napkin over the bowl, and tie this on with string. Bring the opposite corners up two at a time, and tie loosely in a double knot. Now you have a really handsome-looking pudding with a safe and substantial handle.

Check that the water is boiling in the big pan and put in the pudding. Put the lid back on and keep the water boiling gently throughout the cooking time of four hours. Keep an eye on the water level and top up with boiling water from the kettle if needed.

Lift the pudding out of the pan, protecting your hands with rubber gloves, or hooking the stem of a wooden spoon under the knot. Untie it using gloves. Serve the pudding from its bowl with a clean cloth pinned around it and a jug of reduced hot stock as additional gravy.

Serve with very simply cooked vegetables. Carrots and small onions, lightly glazed, are perfect.

venison pasty

Building a mighty game pie in the best English tradition is a satisfying occupation to spread over two or three days. Day one: make and marinate the fillings, and make the stock. Day two: make the pastry, raise, fill and bake the pie. Day three: fill the gaps between pastry and filling with jellied stock. Let the jelly cool and set, then make a start on the pie while the pastry is at its gloriously crisp best. Serves eight to ten.

FOR THE FILLING
1kg venison shoulder, weighed without bone

150ml port

freshly ground black pepper

1 tablespoon juniper berries

750g skinless belly of pork with a good proportion of fat

1 teaspoon anchovy essence

2 cloves garlic, very finely chopped

finely grated zest of an orange (Seville if available)

2 teaspoons salt

FOR THE JELLIED STOCK
1kg game and poultry bones and carcasses

2 carrots, chopped

1 leek, chopped

2 bay leaves

1 teaspoon juniper berries

salt

4 leaves gelatine

4 tablespoons dry Madeira or sherry

FOR THE HOT-WATER CRUST PASTRY
750g plain flour

1 tablespoon salt

1 tablespoon icing sugar

275g butter or lard

300ml water

1 egg, beaten, to glaze

To prepare the filling, trim the venison of every scrap of sinew and silver skin and dice about two-thirds of it into 1cm pieces. Mix the diced meat with the port, a generous seasoning of black pepper and about 1 teaspoonful of the juniper berries, crushed. Cover and marinate in a cool place for 12 to 24 hours.

Mince the remaining venison with the belly of pork. Mix the minced meats with the remaining juniper berries, pepper, anchovy essence, chopped garlic and orange zest. Mix well and refrigerate until needed.

To make the stock, combine all the ingredients, except the alcohol and gelatine, in a large pan and cover with cold water. Bring to the boil and simmer very gently for 3 hours. Cool and strain through muslin, discarding the bones. Simmer to reduce it to 500ml. Salt it to taste.

To make the pastry, sift the flour, salt and icing sugar into a large bowl and make a well in the centre. Put the butter or lard in a saucepan with the water and bring to the boil. Immediately, pour the mixture over the flour, stirring vigorously with a wooden spoon to make a pliable dough. Continue stirring until the dough is cool enough to handle. Turn it on to a lightly floured board and knead until it is smooth. Rest the dough, covered, in a warm place for about 30 minutes.

The traditional way to raise a pie crust is to mould the pastry dough around the outside of a straight-sided glass or stoneware jar. Generously grease the base and walls of the mould with lard or butter, and dust with flour.

Reserve about a fifth of the pastry for the lid and decorations. Spread the larger piece of dough in a rough disc on a baking sheet, flattening an area in the centre to about 1cm thick. Stand the mould in the centre of the dough and mould the dough up the sides of the jar, keeping the thickness as even as possible at around 1cm. Smooth the surface of the walls by rolling them gently with a jar. Trim the top with a knife. Wrap several thicknesses of greaseproof paper bands around the pastry walls to support them, and tie on with string. Chill the dough to firm it.

To extract the mould before filling the free-standing pastry case, put a cloth wrung out in very hot water inside the jar. It will quickly melt the layer of fat on the outside, allowing the mould to be twisted up and out of the dough casing.

Combine the venison, its marinade, the pork and venison mixture, and the salt. Mix well. To test the seasoning, fry a teaspoonful of the filling mixture and taste, bearing in mind that the pie will be served cold so its seasoning needs to be quite bold.

Pack the meat mixture into the pastry case, raising it into a dome above the walls. Roll the reserved dough for the lid into a circle about 1cm thick. Brush the top rim of the pastry with beaten egg before positioning the lid. Press the edges firmly together, crimp the edge and brush the lid with beaten egg. Make a hole in the centre of the lid. Hold it open during baking with a chimney of rolled card. Decorate the pastry lid with re-rolled scraps of pastry. Stick them on with egg glaze and brush with egg to finish.

Bake the pie in a preheated oven, 230°C/210°C fan oven/gas mark 8, for 15 minutes, then cover the pie loosely with foil, reduce the heat to 190°C/170°C fan oven/gas mark 5, and bake for 2½ hours more. Cool the pie completely before removing the papers and chilling it.

Heat the stock. Soak the gelatine and stir it into the stock with the Madeira or sherry. Check the seasoning and allow it to cool. Just before it starts to set again, pour it slowly through a funnel into the pie. Pour in as much as the pie will accept. Chill again to set the jelly. To serve, cut the pie into wedges. Serve with a selection of salads.

pot roast partridge

In midwinter, as the partridge season nears its end, the birds may be less tender than in autumn, and more easily dried out by roasting. Gentle pot roasting ensures both tenderness and succulence. This is also an excellent method for cooking pheasant. Serves two.

1 brace partridge, cleaned and trussed

salt and pepper

2 tablespoons clarified butter

12 shallots, peeled

4 tablespoons Pinot de Charentes, or other white wine

100ml good chicken or game stock

2 slices day-old white bread

clarified butter, olive oil or goose fat for frying the croutons

Season the partridge with salt and pepper. Heat the clarified butter in a small, heavy casserole that is just large enough to hold the birds snugly. Carefully brown the partridge and shallots on all sides. Be careful not to overcook the breast meat.

Add the wine and cook gently, uncovered, until it has almost evaporated. Add half the stock and bring to a simmer. Turn the partridge breast-side down, cover and cook very gently for 20 minutes. Check for tenderness with the point of a sharp knife inserted low down on the breast near the joint with the leg. If the birds are sufficiently cooked, keep them warm until you are ready to serve them. If they need a little longer, add more stock if required, and cook for 10 minutes or so more.

Trim the crusts off the bread and fry in clarified butter, olive oil or goose fat until crisp and golden. Drain on kitchen paper.

Take the breast meat off each side of the birds in one piece, and divide the legs into thighs and drumsticks. Serve each carved bird on its fried bread crouton and divide the shallots and cooking juices between them.

rich venison ragout
with pasta ribbons

1kg venison shoulder, weighed without bone

4 tablespoons olive oil

100g pancetta or bacon, diced or cut into matchsticks

2 tablespoons plain flour

100g chicken livers, chopped

1 carrot, finely chopped

1 onion, finely chopped

2 sticks celery, finely chopped

1 clove garlic, finely chopped

500ml full-bodied red wine

a bouquet garni of thyme, marjoram and bay

1 teaspoon juniper berries

salt and freshly ground black pepper

30g dark chocolate

1kg pappardelle

2 tablespoons butter

freshly grated Parmesan to serve (optional)

A lovely, full-flavoured winter dish to make for two or twenty. It is always worth making a sizeable quantity of the ragout and freezing the surplus in small portions. Fresh egg pasta (see page 20) cut into wide ribbons or squares is a luxurious alternative to dried pappardelle. Serves eight.

Trim the venison of sinew and silver skin and cut into small dice. Heat the oil in a sauté pan or deep frying pan and add the pancetta or bacon. Cook on a medium heat until the fat runs and the pancetta is lightly browned. Remove with a slotted spoon.

Brown the venison quickly in batches, sprinkling each batch with a little of the flour, and follow with the chicken livers. Add the venison and livers to the pancetta.

Lower the heat and add the vegetables to the pan with a little salt; sweat them for 5 minutes, browning them only a little. Return the meats to the pan and pour on the wine. Bring to the boil, add the bouquet garni, juniper berries, salt and pepper. Simmer, covered, for 30 minutes, or until tender. Stir in the chocolate and adjust the seasoning.

Serve on hot plates with freshly boiled, drained and buttered pappardelle. Sprinkle with a little Parmesan if you wish.

roast leg of lamb,
with rosemary, garlic & anchovy

This is too strong a treatment for the first sweet, spring lamb, but there's no better way to cook the meat of more mature animals. The anchovy adds a very attractive and curiously unfishy savouriness to the meat and even more so to the juices. If you can roast on a spit, or over a fire, this is an ideal joint to try. Otherwise, roast in the usual way in the oven. Serves six to eight.

2.5kg to 3kg leg of lamb on the bone

4 salted anchovy fillets, rinsed and coarsely chopped

4 cloves garlic, peeled and sliced

4 sprigs fresh rosemary

salt and freshly ground black pepper

FOR THE GRAVY
500ml good lamb or chicken stock

2 teaspoons cornflour (optional)

Start with the meat at room temperature. To form pockets for the flavourings, use a sharp, pointed knife to make small incisions at regular intervals all over the joint.

Heat the oven to 210°C/190°C fan oven/gas mark 7.

Into each pocket, poke a scrap of anchovy, a slice of garlic and a tuft of rosemary. Season the joint and place it on a rack in a roasting tray. Put the lamb in the oven.

After 20 minutes, reduce the oven to 180°C/160°C fan oven/gas mark 4, and continue cooking – 1 hour more for very pink meat, 1¼ hours for medium, and 1½ hours for well done..If you prefer to take the guesswork out of roasting, use a meat thermometer inserted into the thickest part of the joint (but not touching the bone). It will read 60°C for rare (pink meat); 65–70°C for medium; and 75–80°C for well done.

Nothing will contribute more to the success of a roast, however lightly or well cooked the meat, than to rest it for at least 10 minutes before carving.

Make the gravy while the meat is resting. Pour off the fat. Add the stock to the residual juices in the roasting tray and dissolve them over a medium heat, scraping all the sticky, savoury morsels into the stock. Strain into a small pan, heat and season. To thicken the gravy, mix the cornflour with a little cold water and stir the mixture into the boiling stock. Cook gently for 1 minute. Strain the gravy into a warmed jug.

Baked or roast potatoes and cauliflower in a cheese sauce are good companions for roast lamb.

sauté of lamb
with lemon

Lamb and lemon are happy partners in many guises. This elegant little dish for two demands a lean and tender cut without fat or bones. Small, chunky medallions of meat cut from the loin are just right. Serve them with crushed potatoes, or a velvety purée of potatoes, or with a pile of lightly buttered spinach leaves. Serves two.

1 juicy lemon

½ teaspoon sugar

50g butter

about 300g lamb, in 6 or more pieces

salt and freshly ground black pepper

4 tablespoons dry white wine

Pare the zest of the lemon and cut it into threads. Put these in a small pan with cold water and bring to the boil. Drain and refresh in cold water. Return the blanched zest to the pan with the sugar and 1 tablespoonful of water, and cook until the water has evaporated and the zest is a beautiful bright yellow. Take it off the heat and set it aside. This stage can be done in advance.

Juice the lemon. Heat a third of the butter in a small frying pan. Season the meat on both sides with salt and pepper, and when the butter begins to sizzle, add the lamb and cook it on a moderate heat, turning it once. Timing will depend on the thickness of the pieces and how well cooked you like lamb to be – a little pink is perfect. Remove the meat and keep it warm.

Pour off the cooking butter but do not wash the pan. Add the wine and deglaze the pan over a moderate heat, scraping up the caramelized juices and allowing the liquid to reduce until there is only a scant tablespoonful left. Add a tablespoonful of lemon juice and whisk in the remaining butter to make a small amount of glossy sauce. Check the seasoning.

Arrange the lamb on two warmed plates. Add the meat juices to the sauce. Divide the sauce between the pieces of lamb and garnish each medallion with a pinch of the candied lemon zest.

mushroom
& kidney pies

Light and buttery puff pastry cases are filled with a richly flavoured ragout of mushrooms and kidneys. Putting them together at the last minute guarantees crisp pastry and a tender filling, a combination of flavours and textures that is a delight. These pies are deceptively substantial, so serve them as a main dish with a salad of peppery leaves. Serves four.

FOR THE PASTRY CASES

500g puff pastry, preferably butter puff

1 egg yolk

1 tablespoon milk

FOR THE FILLING

400g calves' kidneys, or 8 lambs' kidneys

50g unsalted butter

salt and freshly ground black pepper

4 tablespoons finely chopped shallot

1 clove garlic, finely chopped

400g mushrooms, wild and cultivated, thickly sliced

50ml dry Madeira

100ml good chicken stock

2 teaspoons Dijon mustard

2 tablespoons double cream

On a floured board, roll out the pastry to a thickness of about 5mm. Cut eight 12cm squares. Place four of the squares on a baking sheet, turning them over as you transfer them. From the centre of each of the four squares left on the board, cut a smaller 9cm square to make the lids. Paint a little water on the surrounding 'frames', turn them over, lay them neatly on the large squares and press gently to secure. With a very sharp knife, score a diamond pattern into the lids and arrange them on the baking sheet. Chill well.

Heat the oven to 220°C/200°C fan oven/gas mark 7. Mix the egg yolk with the milk and brush on the top of the pastry cases and lids, avoiding the edges, which need to puff apart without sticking. Bake for 15 to 20 minutes until the pastry is golden and cooked through.

Make the filling while the pastry is baking. Cut the kidneys into bite-sized pieces, discarding the covering membrane and tough white core.

Heat a wide sauté pan or frying pan and add half the butter. Season the kidneys and add them as soon as the foam subsides. Fry them fairly quickly so that they brown on the outside but are still pink in the centre. Too high or prolonged a heat will toughen them irrevocably. Transfer the kidneys to a bowl and keep them warm.

Add the remaining butter to the pan, then add the shallot and garlic. Fry for a couple of minutes before adding the mushrooms. Cook them quickly so that they colour and reabsorb any liquid they give off. Add the Madeira and continue cooking on a high heat until it has all but disappeared. Add the chicken stock and let it reduce by half. Stir in the mustard and return the kidneys to the pan and mix with the mushrooms. Finally, stir in the cream, taste and adjust the seasoning before dividing the mixture between the four pastry boxes. Put the lids on and serve at once.

pork roasted in milk

There are many variations on this classic Italian recipe for a rib roast of pork slowly simmered in milk that tenderizes the meat and turns to a soft, curdy mass. This is Annie Bell's version, which I have made often, and the crackling has been fragile perfection every time.

Ask the butcher to remove the chine bones at the base of the joint. Ask too for the skin to be scored at .5mm intervals, and sliced off so that the fat is evenly distributed between meat and skin. Serves six.

2.2kg pork loin rib roast, prepared as described

2 tablespoons extra-virgin olive oil

sea salt and freshly ground black pepper

25g unsalted butter

5 garlic cloves, peeled and halved

500ml whole milk

2 bay leaves

Heat the oven to 190°C/170°C fan oven/gas mark 5.

In a roasting dish that will hold the joint relatively snugly, heat the olive oil over a medium heat. Season the meat all over and sear to colour on all sides. Remove it to a plate, pour off the fat and add the butter. Once this has almost melted and is frothing, add the garlic and stir for a moment until it begins to colour. Return the joint fat-side up to the roasting dish, with the chine bones, if you have them, nearby. Pour in the milk, add the bay leaves, bring to the boil and place in the oven.

At the same time, roast the crackling. Rub some salt into the pork skin, place it skin-up in a small roasting dish and put it in the oven.

Turn the heat down to 150°C/130°C fan oven/gas mark 2, and roast for 2 hours, basting the meat frequently. The milk will curdle after about 1½ hours. By the end, the joint should be very golden, sitting in a pool of curds and whey.

Remove the roast to a plate, cover with foil and leave it to rest for 20 minutes. Turn the oven up to 220°C/200°C fan oven/gas mark 7 and continue to roast the crackling while the joint is resting. It should crisp up and turn pale, and be set with small bubbles below the surface.

Just before the end of the joint-resting period, discard the bay leaves and chine bones and reheat the curds and whey, detaching the skin from the sides. Tip the contents into a blender and whizz into a creamy gravy. If this seems overly thick, you can add a drop of boiling water. Taste to check the seasoning, then transfer to a jug.

Carve the roast. You should get one slice between each rib and one with the bone in. Add any juices that flow out to the gravy jug. Drain any fat off the crackling. Serve the roast pork with the crackling and gravy.

vegetables

The way we prepare vegetables has changed more radically in my lifetime than any other branch of home cooking. There are, thank goodness, many more vegetables to choose from. I remember a time when aubergines, peppers, okra, sweet potatoes and coriander had to be tracked down in ethnic shops, when avocados and pumpkins were still a bit of a novelty, and you did not see a fresh pea or green bean from one summer's end until the beginning of the next. Fresh chillies? You must be joking.

Salad was a summer thing. Salad leaves consisted of lettuce, though there was a choice of floppy, cos and, later, iceberg. Since then, a whole dictionary of salad leaves has sprung up – mizuna, mustard greens, rocket, corn salad and 'baby leaves' cropped from plants such as Russian kale, rainbow chard, spinach and dozens more.

Now we take it for granted that there will be year-round supplies of fresh herbs, asparagus, new potatoes, peas and beans flown to a store near us from the farthest corners of the globe. And such is the growers' expertise and the wonders of packaging technology that this cornucopia of fresh produce arrives in our kitchens in pretty good shape. Of course, vegetables that are home-grown and freshly picked taste even better, and if they are organically raised, best of all.

I am also old enough to remember when every lettuce and bag of pea pods came with a cargo of crawling and wiggling insect life that had to be washed off with great care. Chemical sprays have banished small creatures from conventionally grown crops. Organic growers are finding kinder and increasingly effective ways of keeping pests down, which is another reason for choosing organics if you can.

One way or another, everyone now has access to enough fresh fruit and veg to meet the nutritional target of five portions a day, and for vegetarians the increased choice is even more welcome. New cooking fashions have come and stayed around to increase the nation's vegetable-cooking repertoire. Stir-frying was all the rage for a while. It is no

longer a novelty but is still popular. Roast vegetables enjoyed a well-deserved fashion moment and their influence spread widely, leading to new soups, dips and pasta sauces based on the way that dry heat intensifies and concentrates the flavours of raw vegetables. Mediterranean (and particularly Italian) ways of using vegetables, cooking them quickly and simply with rice or pasta, are no longer foreign but mainstream British cooking.

So what happened to our famously soggy cabbage and mushy peas? The jokes about putting the lunchtime vegetables on to boil before the breakfast table had been cleared are the stuff of stand-up gags. In fact, the nation's horror of overcooked vegetables is so great that the hazard now is undercooked vegetables. I mean it.

Can we agree that raw potato, and that includes undercooked potato, tastes horrible, and nothing like fully cooked potato? There are other vegetables that taste better cooked. Asparagus and brussels sprouts are two that are often now served too undercooked to taste even of themselves. And then there are vegetables such as carrots, which can be delicious raw or cooked, but are better cooked through when served in chunks to accompany a steak or a stew. These are, of course, matters of taste. But I do think the fashion for squeaky vegetables has more to do with the caterers' convenience than with thoughtful cookery.

Reading the recipes in this chapter brings back sunny memories of the places where I first tasted so many of the vegetable dishes that make repeated appearances on my table. It was in Provence that I fell in love with basil-scented soupe au pistou, which is great for summer eating. Corsica furnished courgettes baked with a stuffing of fresh ewe's milk cheese and mint, a dish that tastes more fascinating than its few ingredients suggest. Lemon-baked potatoes conjure up the blue of the Aegean and the Greek penchant for serving hot food barely warm, which is handy when the potatoes are to accompany meat or fish from the barbecue. Spiced potato cakes bring back street stalls in the dusty

heat of India, and tarka dhal soup is a reminder of the discovery that spiced lentils can make an enjoyable breakfast.

Winter minestrone, thick with beans and dark with the handsome black cabbage of Italy, is a soup to stand your spoon up in, a rib-sticking meal in itself and one of the most enjoyable ways I know of meeting that five-a-day target. Each bowlful, with its lick of peppery olive oil, evokes a Tuscan vegetable garden in autumn, where cabbages stand proud, there are beans drying on the vine, the last trusses of tomatoes catch a golden afternoon light, and the crack of sporting guns echoes around the hills.

Here, then, are some timeless country dishes that meet our contemporary taste for clear, vivacious flavours, not-too-tricky cooking methods, and healthy eating that is a positive pleasure.

mushroom, leek
& chestnut jalousies

These puff pastry pies, filled with two types of mushroom, would make a satisfying main course for vegetarians in a Christmas menu that includes the usual roast turkey or goose. They contain some of the most popular stuffing ingredients, so if you bake these there is no need to stuff the bird as well. Serves six to eight.

1kg small or medium leeks

100g butter

500g closed-cap or button mushrooms

salt and freshly ground black pepper

2 tablespoons lemon juice

400g cooked, peeled chestnuts

2 tablespoons melted butter

2 large onions, finely chopped

100g wild or open-cap mushrooms, finely chopped

200g fresh white breadcrumbs

4 tablespoons finely chopped parsley

1 teaspoon thyme leaves or ½ teaspoon chopped tarragon

1kg puff pastry, preferably butter puff

1 egg yolk, and 1 tablespoon milk

Top and tail the leeks and cut them into chunks 2cm thick. Steam until almost tender, then transfer to a large bowl and leave them to cool.

Melt 50g of the butter in a wide pan and add the whole closed-cap mushrooms. Sauté them on a high heat until they are beginning to brown. Season with salt, pepper and lemon juice. Fry off any liquid before turning them into the bowl with the leeks to cool. Add the chestnuts and melted butter, season generously and mix carefully so that the leeks and chestnuts do not break up. Set aside until completely cold.

Melt the remaining butter in the pan and add the finely chopped onion. Cook slowly until the onion is tender, but not coloured. Increase the heat and add the finely chopped wild mushrooms. Fry for 2 or 3 minutes until cooked. Take the pan off the heat and stir in the breadcrumbs and herbs. Season the mixture well and set it aside until completely cold.

Roll out half the pastry to a rectangle about 50 x 25cm, and divide it into two squares. Lay one square of pastry on a baking sheet lined with baking parchment and place half the breadcrumbs and wild mushroom mixture in the centre of the pastry, leaving a 3cm margin all around. Pile up half the leek, chestnut and mushroom mixture on top. With a pastry brush dipped in water, dampen the exposed pastry edge.

Cut diagonal slashes in the second piece of pastry and lay it over the first, being careful not to stretch it. Press the edges of the pastry together to seal, trim and crimp. Leave to chill and make up the second jalousie. Just before baking, mix the egg yolk with the milk and paint it on the pastry to glaze, avoiding the edges. Bake in a preheated hot oven, 220°C/200°C fan oven/gas mark 7, for about 30 minutes, until crisp and golden.

soupe au pistou

Pistou is a raw basil sauce, supped across Provence in one of the world's great soups, soupe au pistou. Authentic variations on both soup and sauce are numerous and their merits passionately disputed. This point is very plain, very fresh vegetable soup is wonderfully enriched with pistou at the last moment. It makes one of those summer lunches that is wasted without a glass of wine and followed by a nap. Serves four to six.

To make the soup, bring 2 litres of water to the boil in a large pan and add the potato, haricot beans and leeks. Boil, uncovered, until the haricots are half-cooked. Add the green beans, celery and macaroni. When the macaroni is nearly cooked, add the courgettes and broad beans. Season the soup lightly and continue simmering until all the vegetables and pasta are tender.

While the soup is cooking, make the sauce, ideally using a pestle and mortar, which can go to the table, or a blender. Pound the garlic to a paste with the basil, or blend it. Work in the Parmesan, tomato and 5 tablespoonfuls of olive oil.

Turn the soup into a large serving bowl and stir in a generous spoonful of the pistou. Serve the soup, handing round the remaining pistou separately for everyone to help themselves. For second helpings, stretch the pistou by adding more olive oil.

FOR THE SOUP

2 large potatoes, peeled and diced

300g freshly shelled white haricot beans (or 400g tinned haricot beans, drained and rinsed)

2 medium leeks, tender parts only, chopped

300g green beans, cut into short lengths

2 sticks celery, chopped

100g short macaroni

2 small, firm courgettes, diced

250g fresh broad beans, blanched and peeled

salt and freshly ground black pepper

FOR THE PISTOU

3 cloves of new garlic

4 generous handfuls of basil leaves

100g freshly grated Parmesan

1 large, ripe tomato, peeled and seeded

at least 5 tablespoons olive oil

white bean
& truffle soup

This elegant and simple soup is based on a quickly made, multi-purpose vegetable stock, which can replace meat- or poultry-based stocks in many other recipes. Serves four to six.

FOR THE SOUP
250g dried cannellini beans

1 tablespoon olive oil

1 shallot, finely chopped

1 tablespoon truffle oil, plus a few drops for each serving

FOR THE STOCK
1 tablespoon olive oil

1 medium onion, chopped

2 medium carrots, chopped

1 small parsnip, chopped

3 sticks celery, chopped

100g celeriac, chopped

1 teaspoon salt

1 glass dry white wine

½ teaspoon fennel seeds

½ teaspoon crushed black peppercorns

3 slices dried porcini mushrooms

2 bay leaves and 2 sprigs each of parsley and thyme

Put the beans in a pan and cover them with cold water. Bring to the boil and simmer for 2 minutes. Take off the heat and leave the beans in the water to soak for an hour.

Drain the beans and return them to the pan with fresh water. Bring to the boil, reduce the heat, cover and simmer until the beans are very tender (1 to 2 hours, depending on their age). If you have time, let them cool in the cooking water before draining and using them.

To make the stock, put the oil in a large pan with the onion, carrot, parsnip, celery, celeriac and salt, and sweat the vegetables gently over a low heat for 10 minutes without allowing them to colour. Add the wine, 2 litres of cold water, the fennel seeds, pepper, porcini, bay, parsley and thyme. Bring to the boil, reduce the heat and simmer for 20 minutes. If you have time, allow the stock to cool before straining and using it.

To make the soup, sweat the shallot in a large pan with the olive oil. Cook it very gently for about 15 minutes until it is meltingly soft and the raw onion smell has been replaced by the rich aroma of cooked onion. Add the beans and strained stock. Bring to the boil, reduce the heat and simmer for 5 minutes. Purée the soup using an electric baton whisk or blender, or by pressing it through a mouli-légumes.

Just before serving, whisk in 1 tablespoonful of truffle oil and taste for salt, adding more if needed.

Top each serving with a few drops of truffle oil and serve with crusty bread.

tarka dhal soup

Quick to make and remarkably inexpensive, this lentil soup is a storecupboard standby. Make it as thick or thin as you like. It even travels well in a Thermos. All the Indian breads go well with tarka dhal soup, but best of all are wrap breads toasted whole, or cut into triangles and grilled. Serves six.

500g red lentils

salt

4 tablespoons oil

3 cloves garlic, thinly sliced

¼ teaspoon ground asafoetida

cayenne pepper

TO SERVE
Indian bread or wrap bread

Put the lentils in a large pan with 3 litres of water. Bring to the boil, skim and simmer until the lentils are soft, about 20 minutes.

Blend until smooth and then add salt to taste.

Heat the oil in a small pan. Add the garlic and cook on a medium heat until the garlic begins to colour. Add the asafoetida and fry for half a minute more, then immediately pour the contents of the pan into the soup. Stir and add cayenne pepper to taste. You can blend in the garlic, or leave it floating.

Serve with toasted triangles of wrap bread.

Variation
Substitute 2 teaspoons of cumin seeds for the asafoetida and sprinkle each serving with a generous tablespoonful of chopped coriander leaves.

winter minestrone

It takes a good half an hour's worth of chopping and slicing to prepare the vegetables for this marvellous soup, which is a meal in itself and well worth making in quantity. One ingredient makes a crucial difference and that is the Tuscan black cabbage, cavolo nero. Its leaves have a unique flavour that no other brassica quite matches. Serves ten.

250g dried borlotti or cannellini beans

1 smoked bacon knuckle

bouquet garni of bay, parsley and thyme

4 tablespoons olive oil, plus more to serve

4 large cloves of garlic, peeled and crushed with salt

2 large onions, peeled and chopped

2 large carrots, peeled and chopped

1 parsnip, peeled and chopped

200g butternut squash, peeled and chopped

200g celeriac, peeled and chopped

salt

2 large potatoes, peeled and chopped

4 dried chillies

500g black cabbage, ribs removed, shredded

TO SERVE
peppery extra-virgin olive oil

freshly grated Parmesan

Soak the beans overnight in cold water. Rinse them and put in a large pan with the bacon knuckle and 3 litres of water. Bring to the boil, skim, lower the heat, add the bouquet garni, cover and simmer until the beans are tender.

In another large pan, heat the oil and add the garlic and all the vegetables except the potatoes, plus a teaspoonful of salt. Sweat the vegetables on a low heat without allowing them to colour. Add the potatoes and stir.

Remove the ham hock from its pan and add the beans and stock to the sweated vegetables. Take the cooked ham off the bone, peel off the skin and dice the meat. Add the meat and chillies to the pan and bring to the boil. Simmer until all the vegetables are nearly tender.

For additional flavour, don't hesitate to add pieces of Parmesan rind and the hock skin to the pot, fishing them out just before serving.

Add the shredded cabbage and simmer until it too is tender.

Remove the chillies, bouquet garni, and any additional flavourings from the pan. Purée about 500ml of the soup and stir it back into the pot. Check the seasoning and add more water if it is too thick. Adjust the seasoning.

Serve with plenty of grilled or baked croutons of bread, which have been brushed on one side with olive oil before browning. Let everyone add a splash of peppery extra-virgin olive oil to their serving and a spoonful of freshly grated Parmesan.

Variation
For a quicker version, use tinned beans and substitute cubed bacon or pancetta, sweated before adding the vegetables, for the bacon knuckle.

leek, thyme
& potato gratin

The flavour of thyme and leeks is a time-honoured pairing that has real warmth if the thyme has grown somewhere hot and sunny. Serve the gratin on its own as a main course, or as an accompaniment to plainly grilled or roasted meat. Serves four to eight.

100g smoked streaky bacon, cut into matchsticks

50g butter, or 3 tablespoons mild olive oil

500g leeks, thinly sliced

1 clove garlic, finely chopped

salt and freshly ground black pepper

2 tablespoons thyme leaves, stripped from the stems

1kg potatoes, peeled and thinly sliced

250ml chicken stock

60ml double cream

Put the bacon in a dry frying pan and cook on a low heat until the fat runs. Raise the heat and fry until crisp. Remove the bacon and keep it warm, leaving the fat in the pan.

Add half the butter to the pan followed by the leeks, garlic and seasoning. Cook the leeks gently until they have wilted and are beginning to soften. Return the bacon to the pan and stir in the thyme.

Heat the oven to 200°C/180°C fan oven/gas mark 6, and generously butter a 2-litre gratin or pie dish. Lay an overlapping layer of potato slices in the base of the dish. Top with a layer of leeks, followed by further layers of potato, then leeks, and finish with a top layer of potato. Press to compact the layers, pour in the stock and dot the top with the remaining butter.

Bake for about 1 hour, or until the potato is tender. Pour in the cream, turn off the oven, and return the gratin to the oven for 10 minutes before serving.

festive baked potatoes

Conventionally roasted potatoes are bliss, but soak up a lot of fat and, inconveniently if you have a single oven, need to be cooked at a high temperature for longer than the resting time of any roast meat they will accompany. These part-roasted, part-baked potatoes open up like toast racks. They look good, taste good and absorb much less fat. Serves eight.

16 medium potatoes, about 140g each

100ml olive oil

salt

16 tufts of fresh rosemary, or small sage leaves

Wash and dry the potatoes and heat the oven to 190°C/170°C fan oven/gas mark 5.

The easiest way to make diagonal cuts in the potatoes, without cutting right through, is to first run a skewer through each potato, about 1cm from the base. Make parallel diagonal cuts at 5mm intervals, slicing down to the skewer. Prepare the remaining potatoes in the same way and arrange them side by side, but not touching, on a shallow oven tray.

Just before putting them in the oven, brush them on all sides with oil and sprinkle with salt. Cover the tray loosely with foil and bake for about 1 hour, or until the potatoes are just tender.

Remove the foil and raise the oven heat to 220°C/200°C fan oven/gas mark 7. Brush a little more oil over the tops of the potatoes, insert a tuft of rosemary or a sage leaf into each potato and return them to the oven for about 15 minutes to colour and crisp up.

lemon-baked potatoes

These potatoes are packed with flavour, and because the dish creates its own sauce, it makes a very good partner to plainly grilled or roasted meat, poultry or fish. Serves four to six.

1kg potatoes

200g shallots, finely sliced

4 cloves garlic, peeled and finely chopped

a handful of fresh thyme or oregano

salt and freshly ground black pepper

150ml olive oil

juice of 2 lemons

Heat the oven to 200ºC/180ºC fan oven/gas mark 6.

Peel the potatoes and cut them into walnut-sized pieces. Fill an ovenproof dish or roasting tin with the potato pieces, sliced shallots and chopped garlic. Season with thyme or oregano, salt and pepper, and pour the olive oil over. Add the lemon juice and enough cold water to come a little over halfway up the potatoes.

Bake for a total of about 1½ hours, turning the potatoes over about halfway through cooking and checking that they do not dry out.

spiced lentil
& potato cakes

Serve these filled potato cakes as a light meal with yogurt or chutney, or with a salad. Alternatively, they can accompany plainly grilled meat or fish. The filling can be made with any dried lentils or beans. If you have any cooked pulses handy, allow 100g. Makes ten to twelve.

750g potatoes (a waxy variety such as Charlotte)

salt

50g yellow split peas, soaked

2 tablespoons olive or sunflower oil, plus more for frying

½ teaspoon fenugreek seeds or ¼ teaspoon ground asafoetida

2 tablespoons finely chopped shallot

4 tablespoons finely chopped coriander leaves

1 hot fresh chilli, deseeded and finely chopped

TO SERVE
yogurt

finely chopped coriander leaves

salt

lemon juice

freshly ground black pepper

fresh chilli, finely chopped

Boil the potatoes in their skins until tender. Drain, peel and mash, seasoning to taste with salt only. Cover and set aside.

Boil the split peas in water until they are tender, but not mushy, then drain thoroughly.

Heat 2 tablespoons of oil to shimmering point in a medium-sized frying pan. Add the fenugreek seeds or ground asafoetida and, almost immediately, the shallot. Fry quickly until the shallot colours, then add the chopped coriander and chilli. Fry, stirring for a minute or two before adding the split peas. Reduce the heat, add salt to taste and fry the mixture, mashing it with a wooden spoon until it starts to hold together. Remove from the heat.

Now form cakes of the mashed potato, stuffed with spiced split peas: this calls for a little dexterity. When the potato and split pea mixtures are cool enough to handle, take a spoonful of potato and roll it into a ball about the size of a medium hen's egg, then flatten into a disk in the palm of your hand. Put a teaspoonful of split pea stuffing in the centre and fold the edges of the potato over the stuffing to cover it. Pat it into a neat cake. Shape further cakes in the same way, until both mixtures are used up.

Fry the cakes slowly in small batches, using very little oil, in one or more non-stick frying pans, until they form a rich golden crust, about 10 minutes on each side. Serve hot with a bowl of chilled, strained yogurt mixed with a handful of finely chopped coriander, and seasoned with salt, lemon juice, freshly ground black pepper and, optionally, finely chopped fresh chilli.

stuffed courgettes

Mint, garlic and soft, fresh cheese combine in a fragrant stuffing for baked courgettes. Yellow courgettes are particularly well flavoured. On the Mediterranean island of Corsica, this is a traditional dish in early summer: the mint is gathered wild in the maquis and the fresh cheese is brocciu, made with ewe's milk. Fresh ricotta is a good alternative to brocciu. Serves four.

4 courgettes, about 100g each

250g fresh cheese

1 small egg

1 clove garlic, finely chopped

2 tablespoons finely chopped fresh mint leaves

salt and freshly ground black pepper

1 tablespoon oil

100g fresh white breadcrumbs

Wash the courgettes and halve them lengthways. Hollow out a shallow slot in each using a sturdy teaspoon or, if you have such a thing, a melon baller.

Chop the seedy debris. Mix it with the cheese, egg, chopped garlic and mint, and season the mixture well with salt and pepper.

Divide this stuffing between the courgettes and lay them, in one layer, in a generously oiled baking dish. Sprinkle with the breadcrumbs and bake at 200°C/180°C fan oven/gas mark 6 for about an hour, or until the courgettes are tender. Timing will depend on the size and density of the vegetables. Cover loosely with foil if they are browning too quickly.
Eat hot or warm.

barley couscous
& vegetables

The fiery North African seasoning paste harissa gives this dish of stewed vegetables a subtle, spicy warmth. It is served with couscous made from barley, which has a nuttier flavour than the usual wheat-based varieties. Together they make a most satisfying dish. Serves four.

4 tablespoons olive oil

250g small onions, peeled

3 cloves garlic, peeled and sliced

300g peeled butternut squash, cut into 2cm dice

250g carrots, scraped and sliced into diagonal chunks

250g cooked chickpeas (tinned are fine)

400g tomatoes, peeled and chopped (or tinned tomatoes)

50g raisins

3 tablespoons harissa

salt

2 handfuls fresh coriander leaves, chopped, plus a few sprigs to garnish

225g barley couscous

Heat 3 tablespoonfuls of the olive oil in a large, deep pan and fry the onions until lightly coloured. Add the garlic, squash, carrots, chickpeas, tomatoes and raisins. Stir in 1 to 2 tablespoonfuls of harissa, 1 teaspoonful of salt, and half the chopped coriander. Add about 500ml of water, bring to the boil, cover and simmer very gently until the vegetables are cooked, about 30 minutes.

About 10 minutes before you are ready to eat, put the couscous in a large bowl, pour in boiling water to cover the grain, cover and leave it for about 5 minutes to soak up the liquid. Uncover, fluff up with a fork and stir in 1 tablespoonful of olive oil.

Check the seasoning of the vegetables, stirring in the remaining chopped coriander, and adding more harissa if you like. Serve in wide, shallow soup plates, spooning the vegetables over a mound of couscous. Top each serving with a sprig of coriander.

orange pilau

The inspiration for this rice dish is a fragrant Afghan pilau. It is scented with the zest of oranges (ideally Sevilles), cardamom, saffron, pistachios, almonds and orange flower water. Serve it with grilled or roast quail, game birds, chicken or lamb. Serves four to six.

450g basmati rice

2 tablespoons sunflower oil

2 large onions, peeled and sliced into fine rings

1 large orange (a sour Seville if available)

25g sugar

salt

a generous pinch of saffron

1 tablespoon orange flower water

½ teaspoon freshly ground cardamom seeds

50g flaked almonds, lightly toasted

50g pistachio kernels, halved

Rinse the rice in several changes of cold water and drain. Heat the oil in a large, heavy pan with a tightly fitting lid. Fry the onions slowly, until they are meltingly tender, without allowing them to become any darker than golden brown.

While the onions are cooking, use a sharp knife or vegetable peeler to remove the orange zest, taking none of its underlying pith. Slice the peel into fine threads and blanch these in boiling water for 2 minutes. Drain and reserve the zest.

Add the drained rice to the pan and stir to coat every grain with oil. Pour in 500ml of water and add the sugar, salt, saffron, orange flower water, ground cardamom and the reserved orange zest. Bring to the boil, lower the heat to a simmer, cover tightly and cook for 10 to 15 minutes, or until the rice is tender.

Fluff it up with a fork, mix in the nuts, cover the pan again, and leave to stand in a warm place for about 10 minutes before serving.

roasted butternut
squash with pancetta & pasta

From the cook's point of view, butternut squash is the star of the pumpkin tribe. Roasting brings out the full, sweet flavour of its dense flesh. Add garlic, sage and crisp bacon bits for a pasta dish that is an easy winner. Serves four.

750g peeled and seeded butternut squash, cut into 1cm pieces

2 tablespoons olive oil

3 cloves garlic, in their skins

20 leaves fresh sage

salt and freshly ground black pepper

150g cubed pancetta or bacon

400g fresh egg tagliatelle (see page 20), or 250g dried

75g butter

TO SERVE
freshly grated Parmesan (optional)

Heat the oven to 200°C/180°C fan oven/gas mark 6.

Put the squash, oil, garlic and half the sage leaves in a roasting tray, season with salt and pepper, and mix well with your hands. Roast for 25 minutes, then add the pancetta and roast for another 15 minutes, or until the squash is tender and well coloured at the edges and the pancetta is cooked.

Cook the pasta in plenty of salted boiling water until just tender.

Put the butter in a small pan and heat until it foams. Add the remaining sage leaves and allow them to colour. Squeeze the garlic from its skin and stir into the butter.

Drain the pasta and combine it with the squash and pancetta, and the sage butter. Mix well and serve. You may like to add a sprinkling of freshly grated Parmesan, but try it first without.

sweet & sour onions
with thyme

The flavour of caramelized onions, whether fried, roasted or casseroled, is invariably pleasing. Try this herby sweet and sour version with pork sausages, roast meat or game. Serves four.

500g small pickling onions or round shallots

30g butter

1 tablespoon fresh thyme leaves

50ml cider vinegar or white wine vinegar

1 tablespoon honey

salt and freshly ground black pepper

Peel the onions or shallots, leaving them as intact as possible. The skins will come off much more easily if they are covered in boiling water for a couple of minutes, and minimal trimming will ensure that they hold their shape when cooked.

Melt the butter in a heavy saucepan and add the onions and thyme leaves. Cover tightly and cook on a low heat until the onions are tender.

Uncover the pan and sprinkle the onions with the vinegar and a generous tablespoonful of honey. Season with salt and freshly ground black pepper. Increase the heat and cook carefully until the liquid forms a syrupy glaze. Turn the onions into a serving dish and eat hot or warm.

fish

'Get it up the bank, lassie. Get it up the bank,' a chorus of gruff
voices shouted from the far side of the river. I held the fish pinned
to the long grass, pointing uphill. I don't remember what it felt like
to hook that first salmon, or playing it to the water's edge, but I will
never forget the grip of the hunter's instinct which propelled me into
the shallows to ensure that this was not the one that got away. With
no experience of catching salmon, no landing net, and no gillie
to help, no wonder I was teased for having my fish in a less-than-
ladylike rugger tackle when the yells of the fishermen on the opposite
bank finally summoned my companions.

It was a beautiful fish, a fresh-run hen salmon, silver from the sea,
a good 5.5kg in weight – a perfect fish in fact. The River Dee,
sparkling in early summer evening sunshine, raced on. The gillie,
when he came back, was all for trying again, but I couldn't. One
fish for the pot was wonderful; another would have been greedy.
I cannot properly explain why, because this was at a time when
wild Scottish salmon, although less numerous than they had once
been, were not endangered as they are now.

It will be no surprise that it was the best fish I have ever eaten. The thrill of the chase and perfect freshness are unbeatable seasonings, of course. Just as important, it was an athletic wild fish in its breeding prime. If you want to eat wild salmon with a clear conscience, check the source. In season, wild Scottish salmon, caught by licensed fishermen, is sold by high-class fishmongers and by mail order (see useful addresses, page 144). Wild Alaskan salmon is a less costly alternative, if you can discount the air miles it has clocked up. There are counters and quotas on all the Alaskan rivers, so the evocatively named sockeye, chinnock and coho salmon are a sustainable catch.

By far the best of the farmed salmon I have eaten are the fish reared organically on what the industry calls 'high-energy sites' around the Orkney and Shetland islands off the north-east coast of Scotland. There, fast-flowing tidal waters put physical demands on the fish, making them leaner and firmer than fish reared in quiet lochs and inlets. A slower growth rate on organically approved feedstuffs improves taste, and the flesh is pale because artificial pigments are no part of organic husbandry. Not all organically farmed salmon achieves the highest standards. Some is too flabby and fatty. Conventionally farmed salmon is equally variable, so there is no substitute for shopping around to sort out a reliable supplier.

Of the oily fish that are promoted as a vital part of a healthy and balanced diet because they contain essential fatty acids, organically farmed salmon is the freshest, most readily available, and affordable. Crucially, it is also a sustainable resource (non-organic fish farming being a significant pollutant on some sites). While mackerel, herring, pilchards, sardines and tuna are also rich in desirable fish oils, all are wild fish, and we cannot afford to ignore where and how they are caught if their progeny's progeny are going to be around for our grandchildren to eat.

The Marine Conservation Society's website (see useful addresses, page 144) has all the information required to keep up with the good and bad news on fish. As I write, conscientious consumers can tuck into herring caught in the North Sea, Eastern Channel, Skagerrak, Kattegat and Thames Blackwater fisheries. Though it is another matter altogether whether the chap serving at the fish counter knows his Skagerrak from his Kattegat.

It is hard enough to find sparklingly fresh fish that is really worth cooking and eating, without negotiating an ethical maze, but it is too late to complain. Atlantic cod from overfished waters is off the menu, but Icelandic cod from less exploited stocks is all right. Best at present, and assuming it is actually sold somewhere near you, is organic or certified freedom-farmed cod. Both halibut and turbot are overfished and wild stocks are endangered. But both are also farmed in tanks, not at sea, and fish certified as meeting organic standards ticks all the right boxes.

Farmed shellfish are generally good news too. In fact farmed mussels, clams, king scallops and

oysters top the Marine Conservation Society's list of approved fish to eat. Even the common brown crab of seaside holiday sandwiches can no longer be bought with a carefree lack of regard for its future. In many places these too are overfished, and we are advised to pass up the smallest, which are too young to breed, and the largest, which are the most valuable breeding stock.

If buying fish is a tricky business, at least cooking it is quick and easy. I am happy to leave crisply battered fish in the expert hands of fish and chip shops and pub chefs, and to save deep-fried fish as a treat to look forward to when I'm on the road. The shrimp fritters on page 93 are an exception. The recipe comes from the Atlantic coast of Spain, which is too far to go for a snack.

fresh crab for tea

Eating a fresh crab is not so much a meal, as an event for which newspaper is the best tablecloth. The crab pick and crackers shown in the picture are the proper tools for the job, though there is a long and honourable tradition of using a hammer and a hairpin. Freshness, gender and weight distinguish fine crabs from the rest. Males, which have a narrower flap on the underside, have more of the prized white meat than female crabs. The best crabs are heavy for their size and have very hard shells, both indicators that they have not recently moulted, a process which leaves the flesh inside porous and watery. Away from the quayside, they are invariably sold ready-cooked and should smell sweet and of the sea.

allow 1 cooked crab, weighing about 1kg, per serving

60ml mayonnaise (page 27) made with lemon juice, per serving

salt and pepper

TO SERVE
crusty white bread

The claws are the most generous source of flaky white meat, and there is more in the legs and leg sockets on the body shell. The top shell contains the softer brown meat.

You may want to do some preparation before taking the crabs to the table. Twist off the claws and legs as close to the body as possible. Crack the claws. To open each crab, twist off the bony tail flap on the underside of the body. Then use a small, pointed knife to loosen the join between the top shell and the section the legs were attached to. Pull the underside free, remove and discard the soft, feathery gills along the edges (small boys like to know that these are called the dead men's fingers) and split this part in two with a heavy knife. Go back to the top shell, locate the crab's mouth, and remove and discard the small stomach sack and the appendages immediately behind it.

Now deal out to each diner a top shell, two claws, eight legs, and a body shell split in two. Arm each member of the gathering with a pick, a teaspoon for the brown meat, and a capacious napkin or tea towel. Crackers can be shared. Supply a large bowl for debris and plates and forks for the extracted crabmeat. Put the mayonnaise and seasonings in the centre and set to.

In the unlikely event that there is any leftover crabmeat, use it to make potted crab (page 28), to fill soft brown bread sandwiches, or make the dainty dish which follows on page 82.

rolled omelette
with crab

A conventional omelette, filled with fresh white crabmeat and served straight from the pan, is delicious. This recipe is a little different. It makes bite-sized mouthfuls, each a drum-shaped piece of rolled omelette containing a spoonful of white crabmeat, which are served cold. Offer them singly with drinks, or several at a time with a small salad as a first course, perhaps with assorted toppings. Alternative garnishes can be as simple as a blob of crème fraîche and a wisp of chive or dill. Try flakes of smoked trout or crisp curls of grilled pancetta. Makes 12 pieces.

3 large eggs

3 tablespoons double cream

salt and freshly ground black pepper

1 tablespoon butter

2 tablespoons crème fraîche

100g fresh white crabmeat

12 small sprigs of dill

Heat a medium-sized frying pan or a large omelette pan. Whisk 1 egg with a tablespoonful of cream, salt and pepper. Grease the pan lightly and pour in the egg, tilting the pan to spread it widely and make the thinnest omelette you can manage. Cook it on a low heat until just set, then turn the omelette on to a board and trim the edges square. Roll the square into a cylinder.

Repeat the procedure with the remaining eggs and cream. Trim and wrap each omelette around the first. Roll the resulting three-omelette cylinder in clingfilm and chill it.

Cut the chilled omelette into a dozen rounds and top each with a dab of crème fraîche, a spoonful of crab and a sprig of dill.

roast salmon
with beans & fennel

This is a satisfyingly robust main course dish. Soaking and cooking the dried beans with herbs ensures that they are velvety and infused with flavour. Serves four.

200g dried lima, haricot or flageolet beans

2 lemons

bouquet garni of bay, thyme and parsley

4 chunky salmon fillets with skin

4 small fennel bulbs

100ml light, floral, extra-virgin olive oil

4 tablespoons chopped fennel or chervil leaves, plus 4 sprigs

2 tablespoons finely chopped chives

sea salt flakes and freshly ground black pepper

Soak the beans in cold water overnight. Bring them to the boil in fresh water, skim and add the finely pared zest of 1 lemon and the bouquet garni. Simmer gently until the beans are very tender but not breaking up (1 to 2 hours, depending on the type and age of the beans). Only then, add a tablespoonful of salt and leave to cool in the cooking liquid. Drain, discard the lemon zest and bouquet garni, and put the beans in a saucepan.

Salt the fish and let it stand for 30 minutes before cooking it. Heat the oven to 230°C/210°C fan oven/gas mark 8.

Cut the fennel bulbs, from top to bottom, into 5mm slices. Arrange them in a single layer on an oiled metal baking sheet. Brush with oil, sprinkle with salt and bake for 15 minutes, or until cooked and coloured. Keep warm.

Dry the fish with kitchen paper, brush with oil and arrange, skin-side down, on a shallow baking tray. Roast it, uncovered, for 7 to 10 minutes, depending on the thickness of the pieces.

Add 2 tablespoonfuls of the oil to the beans, together with the finely grated zest of the second lemon. Heat them through slowly and add more salt, if needed, and some black pepper.

To make the herb dressing, mix 1 tablespoonful of lemon juice with ½ teaspoonful of salt, then stir in the remaining oil and chopped herbs.

Divide the fennel slices between four hot plates and top with a spoonful of beans and a piece of fish. Spoon the herb sauce around the beans and the heat of the plates will warm it sufficiently. Finish with a few flakes of salt and a sprig of fennel or chervil.

scampi à la meunière

To cook scampi in the manner of the miller's wife, dipped in flour and fried and sauced with butter, first catch your scamp, which must be raw, shelled and naked of those nasty crumb coatings favoured by the ferret-in-a-basket pub food trade. Good fishmongers sell scampi frozen and ready shelled. Very good fishmongers may offer live Dublin Bay prawns, but then there is the dilemma of despatching them humanely, and jolly sore thumbs from shelling them. For the thrifty cook, deciding what to do with the claws is a further quandry. Shelled frozen scampi are simply the tail meat of Dublin Bay prawns. Serves two.

500g frozen scampi, raw and shelled

100g plain flour

salt and freshly ground black pepper

100g clarified butter (page 27)

50g unsalted butter

1 tablespoon finely chopped parsley

4 lemon wedges

Thaw the frozen scampi carefully, spreading them out in a single layer so that the ice melts evenly. They will be most succulent if they are cooked as soon as they have thawed. If you have to hurry the process, put them in a colander under the cold tap. Avoid keeping thawed scampi waiting to cook, or soaking to thaw them, because it will damage both flavour and texture.

Put the flour and a generous seasoning of salt and pepper into a large paper or plastic bag. Dry the thawed scampi on kitchen paper and put them in the bag. Hold the bag closed and shake to coat the fish with seasoned flour. Remove the floured scampi from the bag, place them on a wire rack and leave them to dry for 10 to 15 minutes. This step helps the flour to form an adhesive coat.

Cooking takes only a few minutes, so heat the plates and get any accompaniments ready – fluffy mashed potatoes are very hard to beat – before starting to cook the scampi. Choose a large, heavy frying pan which will hold all the scampi in one layer. They will need to be turned quickly, so have the tongs or fish slice ready to hand.

Heat the clarified butter in the pan on a fairly high heat. It is hot enough when a trial scampi, dipped into the butter, sizzles immediately. Turn all the scampi into the pan and shake them apart. Let them cook quickly on one side, then turn them over. By the time they have all been turned, they should be almost done. Cut one open, and if it is opaque in the centre, it is ready.

Turn the scampi, now lightly and crisply coated, into a sieve over a bowl, allowing all the fat in the pan to drain through. Spread the scampi on kitchen paper to absorb any excess fat, and divide them between the heated plates. Wipe out the pan with kitchen paper, lower the heat and return the pan to the stove. Add the unsalted butter, and as soon as it has melted, stir in the chopped parsley. Pour this sauce over the scampi and serve at once with the lemon wedges and mashed potatoes to mop up the buttery juices.

Note: the clarified butter left after frying the scampi can be strained through a double layer of muslin and used again for cooking fish.

prawn chowder

Prawn chowder is quick to make and almost a meal in itself. This is fast, fresh, comfort food at its best. There is no need to thaw frozen prawns before adding them to the soup. Serves four to six.

15g butter

100g streaky bacon, finely chopped

2 medium onions, finely chopped

500g potatoes, peeled and diced

250ml chicken stock

750ml full-cream milk

1 bay leaf

salt and freshly ground black pepper

250g small cooked peeled prawns

150ml single cream

2 tablespoons finely chopped parsley

Melt the butter in a large pan and add the bacon. Cook gently until the bacon fat begins to run. Add the onion and continue frying gently until the onion is soft; don't let it colour.

Add the potatoes, stock, milk and bay leaf and bring almost to the boil. Reduce the heat, season, cover the pan and simmer until the potato is soft.

Fish out the bay leaf, add the prawns and cream, and heat gently until the prawns are hot. Be careful that the chowder does not boil at this stage – it would toughen the shellfish and could curdle the soup. Adjust the seasoning and stir in the parsley.

Serve with plain, savoury crackers or crusty bread.

mackerel pâté

Adding softened butter to the already soft, oily flesh of smoked mackerel may appear contrary, but once chilled, it gives the pâté a firmer texture than the more usual crème fraîche or cream cheese. When buying smoked mackerel, look for whole fish in preference to fillets. They are not difficult to bone and the flesh is likely to be more moist and better flavoured. Serves six.

300g smoked mackerel, skinned and boned

3 tablespoons freshly squeezed lemon juice

60g butter, softened

2 teaspoons hot horseradish relish

salt

cayenne pepper

TO SERVE
toast

6 small lemon wedges

Using a pestle and mortar, pound the fish to a smooth paste. Alternatively, use a food processor. Work in the lemon juice, butter and horseradish. Add salt and cayenne pepper to taste. At this stage, the mixture will be fairly sloppy, but it will firm up when chilled.

Spoon the pâté into one large dish, or six small dishes or ramekins, and chill well. Serve with toast and a wedge of lemon. Toasted granary bread is good.

stuffed mussels

Palourdes farcies, a plate of clams bubbling in garlic butter, or a bowl of fragrant moules marinières, mussels steamed with white wine and shallots, are the well-earned reward of weekend sailors who drag their wet and weary limbs up the harbour steps on the other side of the Channel. In this country, fresh mussels are easier to buy than fresh clams, and although these too are farmed in Britain, they are comparatively costly. To make stuffed mussels, choose mussels that are neither too large nor too small – about 4cm long, a little longer than the first joint of your thumb. Serves four as a first course.

48 fresh mussels, plus a few spares

1 shallot, finely chopped

1 clove garlic, finely chopped

150g unsalted butter, softened

3 tablespoons finely chopped parsley

2 tablespoons dry white wine

sea salt and freshly ground black pepper

3 tablespoons dry white breadcrumbs

Make the herb butter first. Combine the shallot, garlic, softened butter and parsley in a food processor and blend until smooth. With the machine running, add the white wine and blend until it has been incorporated. Season the mixture with a little salt and plenty of black pepper. The mussels will be quite salty, so be careful not to overdo the salt.

Wash the mussels and pull off the 'beards', which are the straggly bits they attach themselves to rocks with. Discard any mussels that do not shut when tapped, and any that are broken.

If you are a dab hand at opening live bivalves with a short, sharp knife, go ahead. Discard one half of the shell and leave the mussel meat on the other.

Otherwise, steam the mussels open. Like most shellfish, mussels quickly become tough if overcooked, so the idea is to heat them only enough to make them spring open. They will finish cooking under the grill. Have a pair of tongs ready and a plate to put the opened mussels on. Arrange the mussels in a wide pan, add a couple of tablespoonfuls of water, put on the lid, and set the pan on a high heat. Give it a shake or two, and after a minute lift the lid and have a look. Pick out any that have opened already. Cover and cook a little longer. The rest should now be open. Get them out of the pan and on to the plate quickly, then leave them to cool and twist off the empty half of the shell.

Spread a dab of herb butter on each mussel, followed by a light sprinkling of breadcrumbs. Arrange the mussels on a grill pan and cook them under a very hot grill until the butter is bubbling and the breadcrumbs are lightly coloured. Serve at once – you will need the tongs again – with plenty of crusty bread to mop up the irresistible juices.

salmon pickled in
gin & juniper

Gravadlax is the classic Scandinavian recipe for salmon pickled with salt, sugar, a little alcohol and a lot of dill. It is eaten raw, as thickly or thinly sliced as you like and, especially when it is home-made, is utterly delicious. The work of pickling, or curing, is done by the salt and sugar, which extract liquid from the fish, leaving the flesh denser, firmer and easier to slice.

Other flavour combinations work well, for example fennel seeds, lemon zest and pastis; or pepper, coriander seed and mixed herbs. But far and away the best variation I have come up with is crushed juniper berries with gin and lime zest. This recipe serves six to eight. If you want to double the quantities, cure two pieces of fish sandwiched together, with the skin on the top and bottom of the package.

500g very fresh salmon fillet, with skin

1½ tablespoons sea salt

1 tablespoon light brown sugar

1½ teaspoons juniper berries, fresh or dried

1 teaspoon black or white peppercorns

very finely grated zest of an unwaxed lime

1 tablespoon gin

Choose a thick, middle-cut piece of fish that has been scaled and boned. Check for bones by running a finger against the grain from tail to head, removing any stray bones with tweezers or needle-nosed pliers.

Grind the salt, sugar, juniper berries and peppercorns in a food processor, or work to a fine powder using a pestle and mortar. Rinse the fish in cold water and dry with kitchen paper.

Tear off a large sheet of clingfilm. Rub a third of the salt mixture and lime zest into the skin of the fish. Lay the fish, skin-side down, on the clingfilm and rub the remainder of the mixture into the flesh side. Sprinkle the gin over it. Wrap up the fish in a flat parcel, put it in a flat dish with another dish plus a weight of about 2kg on top, and put it in the fridge. Chill for 36 hours, turning once or twice.

Remove the fish from the fridge and discard the clingfilm and the liquid that has accumulated. Pat dry with kitchen paper and use at once, or rewrap and chill until needed. Pickled salmon keeps for up to a week in the refrigerator: alternatively freeze for up to two months.

Eat it on its own, thinly sliced, with brown bread. Or, better still, eat with warm salad potatoes and a sharpish, mustardy vinaigrette.

tartare of salmon
(fresh & smoked)

When this recipe appeared in a Christmas issue of *Country Living Magazine* as an idea for a smoked salmon first course that could not yet be bought ready-made, a number of readers called the magazine to check that no cooking was required. Not only does it need no cooking, it can be made up to 24 hours ahead. If you like smoked salmon, do try it. Serves eight.

400g well-flavoured smoked salmon

400g fresh salmon fillet, skinned

2 to 3 shallots, very finely chopped

1½ tablespoons mayonnaise (page 27)

salt and freshly ground black pepper

TO SERVE
8 sprigs of chervil or parsley

50g small, tender salad leaves

3 tablespoons balsamic vinegar

3 tablespoons extra-virgin olive oil

Keeping the fish as cold as you can, cut both the smoked and fresh salmon into 3mm dice. Add the shallots and mayonnaise. Mix well, seasoning the mixture to taste.

To shape, place a 6cm ring on a chilled serving plate, spoon an eighth of the mixture into it and press down lightly to compact. Pressing lightly on the fish with the back of a spoon, lift the ring off. Alternatively, place a spoonful on each plate. Repeat for the remaining seven plates.

Chill for at least an hour, or up to 24 hours. Just before serving, top each ring of salmon with a sprig of chervil or parsley. Put a few leaves around it and sprinkle them with a teaspoonful each of balsamic vinegar and olive oil.

shrimp fritters

In the sherry-producing area on Spain's Atlantic coast, tortillitas de camarones are made with very small, live shrimps sold in the markets of Jerez and Cadiz. These crisp, light shrimp fritters have an unforgettable taste of the sea. The batter is made with chickpea flour or a mixture of chickpea flour and wheat flour. Small, peeled cooked shrimps or prawns can be substituted for live shrimps. Serve them straight from the pan with a glass of very cold, very dry sherry. Makes ten to twelve.

70g chickpea flour

70g plain flour

250ml water

1 teaspoon salt

200g small, peeled shrimps or prawns, chopped

2 tablespoons finely chopped dried seaweed or fresh parsley

olive oil for frying

TO SERVE
6 lemon wedges

Sift the chickpea flour and the plain flour into a bowl. Add half the water and whisk until smooth. Stir in the remaining water and salt. Rest the batter for at least 20 minutes in the fridge. It should have the consistency of single cream.

When you are ready to cook the fritters, stir the chopped shrimps and seaweed or parsley into the batter. Pour olive oil (extra-virgin oil is an unnecessary extravagance for frying) into a frying pan to a depth of at least 1cm and heat until it shimmers and just begins to smoke.

The art of making tortillitas is in the frying. They should be lacy and crisp right through. Drop a tablespoonful of the shrimp batter into the oil and, after a second's hesitation, spread it thinly with the back of the spoon. Form as many more fritters as the pan has room for. When the fritters are golden brown on the first side, turn carefully and fry the other side until golden, too. If the batter is too thick, the fritters will be chunky and difficult to cook to a crisp finish without overcooking and toughening the shrimp.

Use tongs to lift the fritters on to several layers of absorbent kitchen paper. Serve at once with wedges of fresh lemon to squeeze over them. Fry the remaining fritters, ideally handing them round as soon as they come out of the pan.

soused herring

This is a Sunday supper dish of my childhood. Choose very fresh fat herring and ask for the fish to be scaled, gutted and filleted in one piece, leaving on the tails – these give the dish a fine, jaunty air. Serves six.

6 fresh herring, filleted

1 large red onion, sliced into thin rings

salt and freshly ground black pepper

1 teaspoon juniper berries

2 small chillies

8 bay leaves, fresh or dried

200ml cider vinegar

Heat the oven to 180°C/160°C fan oven/gas mark 4. Choose a shallow baking dish that will hold the fish neatly when rolled, and is presentable enough to go to the table.

Spread half the onion rings on the base of the dish. Season the flesh side of the herrings with salt and pepper, and roll them up, skin-side out, finishing at the tail. Put the rolled fish side by side in the dish, tails up. Sprinkle with the juniper berries and chillies. Post a bay leaf between each of the fish, and at the ends of the dish. Scatter with the remaining onion rings.

Combine the vinegar with an equal quantity of water and pour it over the fish. Cover the dish closely with greaseproof paper and foil, and bake for 1 hour.

Uncover and bake for another 10 minutes to colour the fish. Cool and then refrigerate. Cooked this way, the herring will keep well for several days.

Eat cold with brown bread and butter, or a freshly made salad of potato and hard-boiled egg, dressed with seasoned soured cream and chopped chives.

roast halibut
with sage butter & capers

Halibut's well-flavoured flesh is firm and succulent. This large, flat fish cuts into thick, meaty steaks that have dark skin on the top and are pale on the underside. Salmon is an alternative choice. The sharpness of the capers cuts the richness of the sage butter. The flavour of little, salted, nonpareille capers is particularly fine. Serves two.

2 halibut steaks, 175g to 225g each

100g unsalted butter

salt and freshly ground black pepper

10 fresh sage leaves (small)

1 tablespoon fresh lemon juice

2 teaspoons salted capers, rinsed

TO SERVE
400g new potatoes, boiled in their skins

lemon wedges

Heat the oven to 230°C/210°C fan oven/gas mark 7.

In a small pan, melt the butter. Brush the fish with melted butter on all sides and season it well with salt and freshly ground black pepper.

Choose a frying pan with a removable or ovenproof handle, and heat it to smoking hot. Add the fish, dark-side down, and sear until well coloured on that side. Remove from the heat, turn the fish and put the pan in the oven for 8 to 10 minutes, until the fish is just cooked.

While the fish is in the oven, heat the butter remaining in the small pan until it foams, and add the sage leaves. When the leaves colour, add the lemon juice and rinsed capers.

Transfer the fish to a warm serving plate and pour the sage and caper butter over it. Serve with plain boiled potatoes and lemon wedges.

baking

Country cooks pride themselves on their baking, whisking up cakes and quiches, bread and biscuits, tarts and pies for summer fêtes, cricket teas, Christmas bazaars, school fundraisers, new church bells, scout halls and scanner appeals. The good causes multiply and so do the demands on our time. So for family meals, social occasions and good works, we need a repertoire of recipes to fall back on – recipes that are quick, easy and reliable. Here are some of my tried and tested standbys.

Making bread is very personal. No other branch of cooking is so often described as therapeutic. It is the kneading, of course. Ten minutes of physical effort on a lump of dough can do wonders for the psyche and the pecs. Better to make a loaf of bread or a fresh pizza than to perform the schoolgirl exercise that accompanied the rhyme 'I must (puff), I must (puff), improve my bust.' Who needs an expensive gym membership when a bag of flour and the kitchen table promise a workout and a meal?

If the keep-fit idea lacks appeal, there is another increasingly popular route to that best of all domestic smells, a loaf in the oven. An electric breadmaker simply needs filling with ingredients and then, like a dishwasher, gets on with the job unaided. Sales of strong flour for breadmaking, and of bread mixes, have rocketed in recent years with the popularity of the machines and, interestingly, organic bread flour now accounts for a sizeable slice of the market – nearly a third.

In my extensive, but by no means exhaustive experience of breadmakers, the recipes supplied with them are designed to produce the maximum volume of bread in the minimum time. What can be wrong with that, you may ask? Only that the end result is not the most interesting bread. The process of allowing the dough to rise is accelerated – yeast is speeded by the addition of sugar and milk powder, to name two often specified ingredients, and the resulting bread tastes less good than bread made more slowly without them.

There are other ways to make breadmaking fit into busy lives. Traditional yeast-raised doughs are less fussy and more obliging than they are reputed to be. They can be chilled in the fridge, which causes them to rise more slowly, but rise they will. They can be frozen, which puts them into suspended animation, and revived at room temperature.

Modern dried yeasts, of the type intended to be mixed first with flour, are wonderfully reliable. All that business of mixing fresh or dried yeast with warm water and sugar, and waiting with bated breath for it to froth into visible life, can be a thing of the past. So, making bread dough is now less troublesome. Another difference between twenty-first-century recipes and those of the recent past is the suggestion that you should use bottled spring water rather than water straight from the tap. This is because chlorinated water inhibits the activity of yeast. Though too much salt can put yeast off its work and too much heat can kill it stone dead, a dough would have escaped the bounds of any known recipe to encounter such extremes.

One of the most fascinating and frustrating things about breadmaking, and indeed all baking, is how variable flours can be, and the impossibility of specifying exactly how much liquid to add. The absorbency of wholemeal flours is especially variable. A bread dough that is too dry will be stiff work to knead, while a dough that is too wet will be impossibly sticky and difficult to handle. Both are easily remedied. Work a little more liquid into the first, and more flour into the second. Then take time to enjoy the feel of the dough in your hands as the kneading action transforms it from a sullen lump to a lively, springy mass. Shape it and bake it, and if it is a loaf, don't forget to get the butter out of the fridge to spread on the crisp heel of the newly baked bread: cook's perks.

Using top-quality butter is one of the most compelling reasons to make your own pastry, and to bake home-made cakes and biscuits. Not just because the results taste incomparably better than the same recipes made with inferior butter or any margarine, but also to control the fats you are eating, in this case not the quantity, but the quality. As the labels of factory-baked products so often testify, oils treated by hydrogenation to turn them into hard fats are commonly used, and these are believed to be the least healthy type of fat.

There is a choice of recipes to make pastry for summer berry tarts: best sweet pastry and almond pastry. Both pastries are good for small tarts, and for making discs of pastry to layer with fruit and cream. But for large tarts to slice, the almond pastry, once baked, is a more robust, practical choice. Fill the baked and cooled pastry cases with a layer of chilled pastry cream (page 19) and top with wild or garden strawberries, raspberries, currants, or blueberries. A little melted strawberry and redcurrant jelly (page 118), drizzled over the fruit, adds another layer of flavour.

brown bread
with oatmeal

Brown bread that is dense enough to make a satisfying sandwich or slice of toast, and springy enough to have some life in it, is the kind I like best. When freshly baked, this loaf has a delightfully thin crust. Oatmeal on its own would not make a good loaf, but adding a small proportion of it to a mixture of wholemeal and white flour makes for excellent flavour. Use medium oatmeal for a nutty texture, or fine oatmeal for flavour alone. Makes two loaves, each weighing about 1kg.

500g strong wholemeal flour, plus more for dusting

500g strong white bread flour

200g medium oatmeal, plus more for dusting

2 sachets easy-blend yeast

1 tablespoon plus 1 teaspoon finely ground salt

800ml hand-hot bottled spring water

1 tablespoon sunflower or olive oil

In a large mixing bowl, combine the flours, oatmeal, yeast and salt. Mix well. Add the warm water and mix to a rough and ready dough. Turn the dough on to a lightly floured board and knead it until it feels soft and springy (about 10 minutes).

Wash and dry the bowl and brush it with oil. Form the dough into a ball, drop it into the bowl and cover it with a cloth or clingfilm. Leave it to rise in a warm, draught-free spot for 1 to 1½ hours.

Lightly oil two 1kg loaf tins, approximately 19cm long by 12cm wide by 9cm high. Turn out the dough on to a lightly floured surface and knead it very briefly for not more than a minute. Divide it into two equal pieces and shape each to fit its tin. Cover and leave in a warm place to rise for another 30–40 minutes, or until the dough has begun to rise above the rim of the tins. Dust the tops with oatmeal.

Turn the oven to its hottest setting, 250°C/230°C fan oven/gas mark 9, and check that the oven shelf is positioned so that the loaves will sit in the centre. Spray a little water into the oven to create a steamy atmosphere for the first phase of baking, and pop in the loaves. Bake for 5 minutes, then lower the oven temperature to 200°C/180°C fan oven/gas mark 6 and continue baking for about 40 minutes. When baked they should have a firm, well-coloured crust and sound hollow when turned out of their tins and tapped on the base.

Now, the difficult bit. Allow the bread to cool completely before slicing.

thin-crust pizzas

Thin crust pizzas work best with fresh, quickly cooked toppings. Choose your cheese. If you like a mild cheese, go for a few slivers of fresh mozzarella curd, or a fresh, soft goat's cheese. For more flavour, try a slice or two of sticky Italian taleggio. Something salty is a must. Add Italian pancetta, home-cured bacon sliced wafer thin, olives or salted anchovies. Add something veggie. Raw asparagus tips are lovely with mozzarella. Slivers of roasted red pepper, wild mushrooms, thinly sliced rings of sweet onion and, of course, halved cherry tomatoes are good choices. And don't forget the herbs. Fresh basil, sage, thyme or oregano are hard to beat. Makes eight individual pizzas, 20cm in diameter.

FOR THE DOUGH

500g unbleached strong white flour

1 sachet easy-blend yeast

2 teaspoons sea salt

¼ teaspoon sugar

300ml hand-hot bottled spring water

2 tablespoons extra-virgin olive oil

To make the dough by hand, put the flour, yeast, salt and sugar in a large bowl. Stir in the warm water, followed by 1½ tablespoonfuls of the oil, and mix to a soft dough. Gather the dough into a ball and turn it on to a lightly floured board. Knead it for about 10 minutes, until it feels silky and springy. Wash, dry and oil the mixing bowl. Put the dough in the bowl, cover with a cloth or clingfilm, and leave in a warm place until it has doubled its bulk (about 1 to 1½ hours).

The easiest way to divide the dough into equal pieces is by weight. For these small 20cm pizzas, you need 8 x 100g balls of dough. When rolling out the dough, keep the remainder covered to stop it drying out.

Half an hour before baking the pizzas, turn the oven to its hottest setting, 250°C/230°C fan oven/gas mark 9. Place a pizza stone or heavy baking sheet in the oven to heat up. Working on a lightly floured board, roll out a 100g ball of dough to make a 20cm disc. A fail-safe way to check the size and transfer it easily in and out of the oven is to lay it on a disc of baking parchment on a baker's peel. To improvise a peel, use a rimless baking sheet or the removable base of a large tart or cake tin.

Prick the dough at approximately 2cm intervals with a fork, brush it lightly with olive oil and cover with clingfilm. Leave it to rise for about 15 minutes.

Put the toppings on the dough with a light hand. Brush them with a little olive oil and slide the pizza into the oven on its paper. Bake for 7–10 minutes and slide it out on its paper, on to a heated plate. Whisk out the paper, and eat the pizza at once. A splash of chilli-flavoured oil goes well with pizza.

best sweet pastry

This very rich, very light pastry is too fragile for big tarts, but it makes the best small tart cases and flat biscuits to layer with soft fruit. It can be baked blind, without paper and beans, provided that it is well chilled or cooked straight from the freezer. This means that it is possible to have a supply of frozen tart cases ready to bake. The ideal size for tart cases for individual desserts is 10cm: use loose-bottomed 10cm tart tins lined with thinly rolled pastry. Makes six 10cm tart cases.

150g plain flour

50g icing sugar

¼ teaspoon salt

100g unsalted butter, diced

1 egg yolk

½ teaspoon vanilla extract

To make the dough by hand, lightly mix the dry ingredients together in a large bowl. Add the diced butter and rub it in with your fingertips. Combine the egg yolk and vanilla extract, and mix with the dry ingredients to form a dough.

To make the dough in a food processor, put the flour, sugar and salt into the goblet and whizz briefly. Add the diced butter and process in short pulses until the ingredients are the texture of fine breadcrumbs. Mix the egg yolk with the vanilla extract, add to the dry mixture and process briefly until it forms a ball of dough.

Turn the dough on to a floured board, shape it into a cylinder, wrap and chill.

To line the tart tins, cut off discs of dough and roll out lightly on a floured board. Press the dough into the tins without stretching it. Chill before baking, or freeze until needed.

Heat the oven to 180°C/160°C fan oven/gas mark 4. Arrange the filled cases on a baking sheet and bake for 10–12 minutes, or until golden. Transfer the baked cases to a cooling rack and allow the pastry to cool to lukewarm before carefully removing the tins.

almond pastry

Don't even think about trying to roll out this dough. It is more easily pushed into shape with your fingertips. Almond pastry is especially good with strawberries. Vary the recipe with toasted ground hazelnuts in place of the almonds for tarts filled with raspberries or peaches. Makes two 20cm, one 28cm or ten 10cm tart cases.

250g plain flour

¼ teaspoon salt

75g icing sugar

50g ground almonds

finely grated zest of ½ orange

250g unsalted butter, chilled and diced

2 egg yolks

1 tablespoon brandy or water

To make the dough by hand, lightly mix the dry ingredients together in a large bowl. Add the diced butter and rub it in with your fingertips. Combine the egg yolks and brandy or water and mix with the dry ingredients to form a dough.

To make the dough in a food processor, put the flour, salt, sugar, ground almonds and orange zest into the goblet and whizz briefly. Add the diced butter and process in short pulses until the ingredients are the texture of fine breadcrumbs. Mix the egg yolks with the brandy or water, add to the dry mixture and process briefly until it forms a ball.

Turn the dough out on to a lightly floured board and form it into a cylinder, then wrap and chill well.

Cut 5mm-thick slices from the cylinder of dough and lay them, overlapping a little, on the base and walls of the tin (or tins). Then use your fingers to press the pastry into shape, aiming for an even thickness over the base, and slightly thicker edges which reach the top of the sides of the tin. Chill or, better still, freeze the tart cases.

Heat the oven to 180°C/160°C fan oven/gas mark 4. Place the filled case or cases on a baking sheet and bake for 10–20 minutes or more. Timing will depend on the size and thickness of the pastry cases, and whether they are baked from frozen.

Transfer the baked cases to a cooling rack and allow the pastry to cool to lukewarm before carefully removing the tins.

strawberry strudels

Turn the texture of firm strawberries to advantage by baking them, apple fashion, in these scrumptious strudels. Serve them hot or warm with a spoonful of thick Greek yogurt. Makes twelve.

500g firm strawberries, hulled

100g caster sugar

100g ground almonds

100g fresh brioche crumbs or breadcrumbs

1 teaspoon finely grated orange zest

2 tablespoons strawberry or raspberry liqueur, kirsch or brandy

12 sheets of filo pastry, approx. 30 x 20cm

100g butter, melted

caster sugar to dust

Heat the oven to 180°C/160°C fan oven/gas mark 4. Prepare one or more swiss roll tins by brushing the base and sides with melted butter.

Dice the strawberries into approximately 1cm cubes and place in a bowl with the sugar, almonds, brioche crumbs, zest and alcohol. Mix lightly to distribute the ingredients evenly.

Take one sheet of filo pastry and lay it down with a short side closest to you. Brush it liberally with melted butter. Put a generous spoonful of the strawberry filling on the dough in a sausage shape, close to the edge nearest you, leaving a margin of about 2cm at either side. Roll up the pastry loosely in a cylinder, folding in the side margins after a turn or two. Lay the filled strudel seam-side down on the prepared baking tray.

Use the remaining pastry and filling to make eleven more strudels, setting them side by side (not quite touching) on the baking trays. Brush the tops with melted butter, dredge with caster sugar and bake for about 35 minutes, until lightly browned and crisp on top.

Lady Jekyll's
orange jumbles

Agnes, sister of the famous gardener Gertrude Jekyll, wrote cookery articles for *The Times* in the 1920s. This is her recipe for crisp orange and almond biscuits to serve with glasses of fruit and cream. Makes about twenty-four.

85g softened butter

115g caster sugar

115g shredded almonds

55g plain flour

finely grated zest and juice of 2 oranges

Heat the oven to 160°C/140°C fan oven/gas mark 3. Cream the butter and sugar together, then mix in the almonds, flour, orange zest and about 3 tablespoonfuls of the juice, to make a mixture which is soft but not floppy.

Place teaspoonfuls of the mixture on baking sheets lined with baking parchment, spacing them well apart.

Bake for 15–20 minutes until all of the biscuits are a light golden brown. Allow them to cool a little on their papers before transferring them to a wire rack. They should be thin and brittle.

oatmeal biscuits

Freshly baked oatmeal biscuits taste buttery and wholesome and nothing goes better with a selection of prime British cheeses. Makes about twelve.

55g fine oatmeal

175g unbleached white flour

2 level teaspoons baking powder

½ teaspoon salt

100g chilled butter, diced

2 tablespoons caster sugar

3 tablespoons milk

Put the oatmeal, flour, baking powder and salt into a food processor and whizz together. Add the butter and sugar and process until the mixture resembles fine breadcrumbs. Add the milk and process briefly to a dough. Alternatively, make the dough by hand. Put the dry ingredients in a large bowl and mix. Add the butter and work the mixture with your fingertips until it resembles fine breadcrumbs. Add the milk and form into a dough.

Rest the dough for 15 minutes, and heat the oven to 200°C/180°C fan oven/gas mark 6. Roll out the dough to a thickness of 4–5mm, using plenty of oatmeal to prevent sticking. Cut it into neat 8cm squares and set them on non-stick baking sheets. Prick each biscuit five or six times across the diagonal with a fork. Bake for about 12 minutes, until lightly coloured. Rest the biscuits on their baking sheet for a minute or two before transferring them to a wire rack to cool. When they are completely cold, store in an airtight container.

burnt honey
& orange drizzle cake

Caramelizing the sugars in honey adds yet another layer of flavour to honey's already complex taste – although it would be a waste to give this treatment to the finest honey from a single flower source, such as heather or clover.

250g self-raising flour

¼ teaspoon salt

150g unsalted butter, chilled

finely grated zest of 1 orange

200g honey

1 large egg

2 tablespoons milk

FOR THE TOPPING
100g honey

4 tablespoons freshly squeezed and strained orange juice

Line a 12 x 18cm loaf tin with baking parchment and heat the oven to 180°C/160°C fan oven/gas mark 4.

Sift the flour and salt into a mixing bowl and rub in the butter, using your fingertips, until the mixture resembles fine breadcrumbs. Or use a food processor to combine the flour, salt and butter, then transfer the mixture to a mixing bowl. Lightly stir in the finely grated orange zest. In a bowl or processor, combine the honey, egg and milk, and whisk or process briefly.

Combine the wet and dry ingredients and mix them lightly and thoroughly together. Turn the mixture into the prepared tin and spread the top flat. Bang the tin sharply on a flat surface to settle the mixture.

Bake the cake in the centre of the preheated oven for about 70 minutes, or until a skewer inserted into the centre of the cake comes out clean.

Take the cake out of the oven. Allow it to cool for 10 minutes before taking it out of the tin and removing the baking parchment. Set it on a wire rack with a dish underneath.

Make the burnt honey topping as soon as the cake comes out of the oven. Put the honey in a small, heavy saucepan and bring it to the boil. Continue heating it, watching it carefully. Soon, the extraordinary, flowery, honey smell will be joined by the unmistakable smell of caramel. Take the pan off the heat immediately and plunge the base briefly into cold water. Add the orange juice to the caramel in the pan and set it over a low heat. It will soon dissolve again.

Strain the warm burnt honey syrup. Spoon it over the top of the warm cake and paint it over the sides. Use about half the syrup, let it soak in, then use the other half. Finally, spoon the drips collected underneath back over the cake.

Serve the cake at teatime, or as a pudding with thick cream or yogurt.

hazelnut
meringue biscuits

If you like ratafias and amaretti biscuits, try these, made with hazelnuts. Serve them with tea, with after dinner coffee, with ices, or soaked in booze at the bottom of a trifle. Makes about fifty.

150g shelled hazelnuts

2 large egg whites

150g icing sugar, sifted

Heat the oven to 150°C/130°C fan oven/gas mark 2. Use a food processor to grind the hazelnuts to the consistency of very fine breadcrumbs.

Whisk the egg whites until they hold soft peaks. Add half the sugar and whisk until the meringue holds stiff peaks, then fold in the ground hazelnuts and the remaining sugar. Mix to a soft, sticky dough. Spoon or pipe the mixture in small mounds (a teaspoonful or less) on baking sheets lined with non-stick baking parchment. Space the biscuits to allow for a small amount of spreading.

Bake the biscuits for about 45 minutes, or until they are quite dry and a pale, pinkish brown. Leave on the paper to cool on a wire rack. When they are quite cold, peel off the baking parchment. Store the biscuits in an airtight container, where they will keep well for several weeks.

sponge finger biscuits

These are also known as boudoir biscuits. Use them in trifles and for whim-whams (page 138). Makes about thirty.

3 eggs, separated

75g caster sugar

1 teaspoon orange flower water

75g plain flour

sifted icing sugar to dust

Heat the oven to 170°C/150°C fan oven/gas mark 3 and line two or more oven trays with baking parchment.

Whisk the egg yolks and sugar until pale and fluffy. Whisk in the orange flower water, then fold in the flour.

In another bowl, and using a clean, dry whisk, whisk the egg whites until they hold stiff peaks. Fold one large spoonful of the beaten egg white into the first mixture, and when it is well blended, fold in the remainder.

Use a piping bag fitted with a plain 9mm nozzle to pipe 10cm-long fingers

Use a piping bag fitted with a plain 9mm nozzle to pipe 10cm-long fingers on the prepared baking sheets, leaving space for the biscuits to spread a little. Dust them with icing sugar.

Bake the biscuits in the preheated oven for 20 minutes, taking care that they do not take on too much colour. Turn the biscuits over and bake them for another 5 minutes before removing them from the oven to cool on a wire rack.

butterscotch
shortbread

Unrefined light muscovado cane sugar and best butter give this shortbread its particularly rich flavour. Makes eight pieces.

125g unsalted butter, softened

50g light muscovado sugar

½ teaspoon vanilla extract

¼ teaspoon salt

150g plain flour

25g ground almonds

caster sugar for sprinkling

Cream the butter and sugar until light and fluffy. Blend in the vanilla extract and salt, then gradually work in the flour and ground almonds until completely blended.

On a baking sheet, shape the dough into a circle, pressing and patting it to a diameter of about 25cm. Pinch the edge decoratively and prick all over with a fork. Chill the dough for at least an hour before baking.

Heat the oven to 160°C/140°C fan oven/gas mark 3. Bake the shortbread for 30–35 minutes, or until the top feels firm. Leave it to cool for about 10 minutes on the baking sheet or in its tin, before cutting it into wedges and sprinkling with sugar. When it is completely cold, store the shortbread in an airtight container.

preserves

What is it about jam-making that is so pleasing? Is there more to it than satisfying our squirrel-like instinct to fill a few shelves with stores against a rainy day, or the undeniable gratification of cooking anything that does not vanish at the next meal? Of course there are no nicer ingredients to work with than fruits, a sensuous succession of currants, berries, peaches, nectarines and plums. Nor is there any simpler alchemy than combining fruit, sugar and heat to produce jewel-like jars filled with the scents and tastes of summer. I cannot spread a spoonful of raspberry jelly without reliving a midsummer morning spend picking the berries in sight of the South Downs, with gangs of mewing adolescent swifts practising dashing aerial manoeuvres overhead.

Another of the pleasures of preserving is being in the kitchen, exercising the unchanging craft of generations of cooks for whom there would have been no jam tomorrow if they had not made jam today. Methods have hardly changed in 400 or more years. Note these instructions from *Delights for Ladies*, first published in 1600, for making a conserve of damsons. 'Take a pottle of damsons: prick them, and put them into a pot, putting thereto a pint of rose-water or wine, and cover your pot: let them boile well: then incorporate them by stirring and, when they be tender, let them coole, straine them with the liquor also: then take the pulp, and set it over the fire, and put thereto a sufficient quantity of sugar, and boil them to their height or consistency, and put in gally pots or jarre glasses.'

In Tudor England, the point of preserves was just that, to lay up stores of food in seasons of plenty to be called upon during the unproductive winter months. Now we make them not of necessity, but for the fragrant flavours that home-made jams, jellies and conserves will always have when made with fresh fruit and a generous hand.

Making marmalade brings a burst of Mediterranean sunshine into midwinter kitchens. A magical marriage is made when the astringent, mouth-puckering juice and highly scented bitter peel of Seville oranges meet sugar. As seasonal rituals go, marmalade-making is a robust survivor. Perhaps the brief season for Sevilles, a few weeks from the end of January through February, acts as a spur. Although oranges can be frozen whole, so we can, theoretically, make marmalade at any time of year, fresh oranges are much nicer to work with than slippery defrosted fruit.

I delight in the craftsmanship involved in making marmalade as beautifully as possible, aiming for evenly hand-cut peel suspended in a translucent and not too stiffly set gel. A really sharp knife to slice the peel, and an old-fashioned wooden reamer to scoop out all the flesh, pips and pith with a single turn of the wrist, are the only kit required. They will do a better job, too, than mincers or processors.

Making preserves successfully depends on getting a succession of steps right. Here are the most important ones. The better the fruit, the better the flavour of the final preserve. Really ripe fruit is highly perfumed and complex. Always discard any bruised or mouldy bits. Berries, in particular, should be picked in dry weather.

The type of sugar to use depends on the result required. For sparkling clear jellies, I use preserving sugar, which has large crystals and looks like dishwasher salt. It is not to be confused with jam sugar, which has added pectin for a fail-safe set, but gives a different, less silky texture. For jams, conserves, marmalade and curds, I use unrefined organic sugar. Always be particularly careful that the sugar has dissolved completely before boiling for a set, or it may crystallize later in the finished preserve. Wash down any crystals from the sides of the pan with a brush dipped in water.

Resist the temptation to double quantities unless you are sure your pan is big enough. The traditional shape of a preserving pan is wider at the top for efficient evaporation, and quite deep to allow the boiling jam to rise up the pan when it reaches a rolling boil. To test for setting point, which is usually reached after 10 minutes or so of rapid boiling,

drop a little of the preserve on to a chilled plate. If it thickens and forms a skin almost immediately, it will set. As soon as setting point has been reached, remove the pan from the heat and skim off any froth at once.

Jars must always be spotlessly clean, dry and warm. Heat them in a very cool oven (110°C/100°C fan oven/gas mark ¼) before filling. Jellies are best potted in small jars; take care not to move the jars while the jelly is setting or it may split.

Lids or covers should be applied either when the preserve is boiling hot, or when it is completely cold. Never cover warm pots, because condensation will form under the lids and can lead to mould. Put a clean cloth over cooling jars waiting for their lids or covers.

To keep your preserves in top condition, store them somewhere cool, dry and dark. Curds should be refrigerated.

strawberry
& redcurrant jelly

Strawberries have little acidity, and too little pectin, to make a good jelly on their own. The advent of sugar with added pectin for making preserves solves the problem, and the acidity of redcurrants enhances the flavour. A spoonful of strawberry and redcurrant jelly with a warm, buttery croissant is a feast. Melted and brushed or dribbled over the berries on a home-made strawberry tart, the jelly gives a dramatic flavour boost. It is well worth making double or triple quantities if there is a glut of strawberries in the market, or helping hands at the pick-your-own farm. Makes about 1kg.

1kg ripe strawberries

300g redcurrants

juice of 1 lemon, strained

about 500g pectin-enriched sugar

Roughly chop the strawberries and put them into a pan with a heavy base. Strip the redcurrants from their stalks and add them to the pan with the lemon juice. Heat gently, crushing the fruit against the side of the pan to encourage it to release its juice. Bring slowly to a simmer and cook until the fruit is soft.

If you have a jelly bag, pour a kettleful of boiling water through it before tipping in the fruit and letting it drip overnight into a bowl or large measuring jug. Alternatively, strain through a large sieve lined with three or four layers of muslin. Resist the temptation to squeeze the bag to extract the last possible drop of juice, because it could result in a cloudy jelly.

Measure the strawberry and redcurrant juice and pour it into a clean pan. Add warmed sugar, allowing 75g of sugar to every 100ml of juice (750g to 1 litre). Heat gently until the sugar has dissolved completely, then bring the liquid to a rolling boil that cannot be broken down when stirred. Boil for 4 minutes, remove from the heat, skim any froth from the surface and pour gently into warmed, sterilized jars. Cover immediately, or when completely cold.

raspberry jelly

It helps to have a rampant raspberry patch to make raspberry jelly, an extravagant preserve that distils a basketful of fruit into a few small jars. There isn't a better-tasting or prettier jelly – sheer heaven with a warm, buttery croissant or toasted brioche. Keeping the fresh intensity of the fruit means accepting a lightly set jelly. Makes about 1kg.

2kg ripe raspberries

strained juice of 4 lemons

about 750g sugar

Put the raspberries in a large, heavy-bottomed pan and add the lemon juice. Heat slowly – just enough to make the fruit give up its juice while keeping the freshest possible flavour – and as it begins to release its juice, break it up to encourage more.

If you have a jelly bag, pour a kettleful of boiling water through it before tipping in the fruit and letting it drip overnight into a bowl or large measuring jug. Alternatively, strain through a large sieve lined with three or four layers of muslin. Resist the temptation to squeeze the bag to extract the last possible drop of juice, because it could result in a cloudy jelly.

Measure the juice and pour it into a preserving pan. Add 75g sugar for every 100ml of juice (that's 3 parts of sugar to 4 parts of juice). Heat slowly, stirring until the sugar has dissolved completely, then increase the heat and boil for a set. Start testing after 5 minutes. As soon as the setting point is reached, take the pan off the heat, skim off any froth, and immediately pour the jelly into heated jars. Small jars are best. Cover them immediately with jam pot covers or lids, and leave them undisturbed until the jelly is quite cold and set.

rowan
& crab apple jelly

Rowans, the brilliant orange berries of the rowan or mountain ash tree which grows all over Britain, are too sour and bitter to be eaten raw, except by the birds. Scots have traditionally made them into an excellent jelly to serve with game, especially grouse and venison. It is good too with mutton, lamb and goose. Adding apples improves the set of the jelly and also the flavour. Rowans on their own are just a bit too bitter. Use cooking apples instead of crab apples if you wish. Makes about 1kg.

500g rowan berries

500g crab apples

about 500g sugar

Remove the rowan berries from their stalks and wash well. Cut up the apples roughly (there is no need to peel them or to remove the cores) and place both fruits in a pan with just enough water to cover them. Simmer gently for about 45 minutes, or until the fruit is very soft, crushing it with a potato masher.

If you have a jelly bag, pour a kettleful of boiling water through it before tipping in the fruit and letting it drip overnight into a bowl or large measuring jug. Alternatively, strain through a large sieve lined with three or four layers of muslin. Resist the temptation to squeeze the bag to extract the last possible drop of juice, because it could result in a cloudy jelly.

Measure the juice and pour it into a large, clean pan – the traditional wide preserving pan is ideal. Add warmed sugar, allowing 75g to every 100ml of juice. Heat gently until the sugar has dissolved completely, then bring the jelly to a rolling boil that cannot be broken down when stirred. Boil for about 10 minutes or until setting point is reached.

Skim the jelly and pour it, very gently, into warmed jars. Don't pour too quickly because this will create bubbles in the jelly. Cover immediately, or when completely cold.

Variations
Blueberries or blackberries can be substituted for the rowans to make excellent jellies on the same foundation of crab apples or cooking apples. Crab apples make a pretty pink jelly in their own right, which is delicately flavoured and an ideal base for jellies infused with fresh herbs.

rhubarb
& vanilla jam

The addition of vanilla gives a tantalizing new dimension to the flavour of rhubarb jam. Spread the jam lavishly and top with crème fraîche as a filling for buttery sponge cakes or freshly baked scones. Although rosy stalks of forced winter rhubarb make a prettier pale pink jam than coarser summer rhubarb, which cooks to a pinkish shade of brown, the summer fruit gives a better set. Makes about 1.25kg.

1kg summer rhubarb, trimmed weight

1 vanilla pod

1kg sugar

Wash the rhubarb, cut the stalks into short lengths and put them in a big bowl. Split the vanilla pod lengthways and run a knife tip down its inside length to extract the sticky black seeds. Add the seeds and split pod to the fruit. Now stir in the sugar, cover the bowl and leave it in a cool place, ideally not the fridge, for 8 hours or more (24 will do no harm). When you go back to it, the sugar will have drawn an enormous amount of juice from the rhubarb and the vanilla will perfume the fruit.

Transfer the contents of the bowl to a preserving pan and heat, stirring gently, until the sugar has dissolved completely. Then bring to the boil and boil briskly for a set. The vanilla seeds will produce an evil-looking froth of scum, which can be skimmed off without spoiling the flavour.

When setting point is reached, remove the vanilla pod, and let the jam stand for 5 minutes before potting it in hot jars. Cover the jars with a clean cloth and let them become completely cold before putting on lids or papers.

scotch marmalade

A dram of whisky adds a little luxury to a classic medium-cut marmalade. It is optional of course, but it won't send the children reeling from the breakfast table because the alcohol vaporizes immediately on contact with the boiling hot jam, leaving behind only a little extra flavour. Makes about 2.6kg.

1kg Seville oranges

juice of 1 lemon

2 litres water

2kg preserving sugar

75ml whisky

Set a large sieve over a bowl and line it with a double layer of muslin. Working over the sieve, juice the oranges and lemon with a reamer, scouring out the shells as you go and dropping all the pips, membrane and loose pith into the sieve.

Tie the residue into a loose bag with string and put it in a large pan with 2 litres of water and the strained juice.

Discard the shell of the lemon. Halve the orange shells before slicing them finely. Add the peel to the pan, bring to the boil and simmer for 2 hours, or until the peel is meltingly tender. Once the sugar is added, it will not soften further.

Remove the bag and squeeze as much liquid out of it and back into the pan as you can. Discard the contents of the bag.

Add the sugar to the pan and heat, stirring gently, until the sugar has dissolved completely. Increase the heat and boil rapidly for a set – about 15 minutes.

When setting point has been reached, take the pan off the heat, stir in the whisky and allow the marmalade to cool for 10 minutes, then stir again before potting it in warm jars. Cooling allows the marmalade to thicken a little and hold the fragments of peel suspended evenly in the jar. Cover with a cloth until cold, then apply lids or covers.

Seville orange curd

Seville orange curd is a spread with attitude. Curds made with eggs do not have the long keeping qualities of other preserves. They are best made in small batches, stored in the refrigerator and eaten quickly. Makes about 500g.

3 Seville oranges

1 lemon

250g caster sugar

125g unsalted butter

2 very fresh eggs

Wash and dry the oranges and lemon. Using a very fine microplane grater, take the zest off the oranges. Put it in the top of a double boiler, or in a pan which will sit steadily over a pan of water. Add the strained juice of the oranges and lemon, the sugar and butter.

Whisk over a pan of hot, but not boiling, water until the sugar has dissolved. Beat the eggs and strain them into the orange mixture. Cook, stirring until the mixture is just thick enough to coat the back of a wooden spoon.

Pot in warmed jars. The curd will thicken further as it cools. When quite cold, apply lids or paper covers.

strawberry curd

Strawberries with plenty of flavour are needed for this unusual curd. The curd makes a rich filling for cakes and roulades. Makes about 650g.

200g strawberries

finely grated zest of 1 orange

finely grated zest and juice of 1 lemon

300g caster sugar

120g unsalted butter, cubed

4 very fresh eggs

2 tablespoons grenadine syrup (optional for colour)

Wash and dry the strawberries, then hull them. Purée the berries and, if you like, sieve out the pips.

Put the the strawberry purée in the top of a double boiler, or in a bowl sitting over a pan of simmering water. Add the zest and lemon juice, the sugar and the butter. Beat the eggs and add them to the bowl. Stir and add the grenadine for extra colour if you like.

Cook, stirring, until the sugar dissolves; then continue cooking, stirring often, until the mixture thickens.

Pour the curd into warm, spotlessly clean jars, cover with a cloth and leave until cold before closing with jam pot covers or lids.

desserts

...or puddings if you prefer, but anyway this chapter concerns that essential something sweet that ends a meal and without which no meal seems quite complete. This is, without apology, a full-fat, real sugar, high-satisfaction zone that has no truck with 'lite', 'low in', or artificial. And that is because I know for a fact that a couple of spoonfuls of something real and gorgeous is truly satisfying in a way that an eye-popping portion of air and illusion never can be. So come on, let's make lovely puddings. All but one include fresh fruit.

Trifles and whim-whams are party puddings. Their names speak of frivolity and festivity, and their common history is a blur of booze, biscuits, custard and cream. Although the first published recipe to flaunt the label 'trifle' was a poor affair recorded at the close of the sixteenth century — nothing more than a kind of sweet clotted cream flavoured with ginger and rosewater — it evolved into layered extravaganzas laced with alcohol and strewn with comfits.

Fine manchet bread soaked in sack (typically sherry, but also Canary and Malaga wines) and topped with a custard of thick cream, egg yolks, sugar, mace and rosewater, made a two-layer trifle in the middle of the seventeenth century. A hundred years and another layer later, Hannah Glasse wrote: 'Cover the bottom of your dish or bowl with Naples (sponge) biscuits broke in pieces, mackeroons broke in halves, and ratafia cakes; just wet them all through with sack, then make a good boiled custard, not too thick, and when cold pour it over it, then put a syllabub over that. You may garnish it with ratafia cakes, currant jelly, and flowers, and strew different coloured nonpareils over it.'

At around the same time, north of the border in Scotland, another writer, Elizabeth Cleland, was soaking sponge biscuits in the sweet wine of Malaga, covering them with custard flavoured with cinnamon and orange zest, and topping her trifle with apple snow – a froth of roast apples mixed with meringue and whipped up 'very high'. This had the economical merit of using both egg whites and yolks in the same dish. Trifle is an adaptable survivor, made lavishly in times of plenty, and with

thrifty ingenuity when times are hard. Elizabeth Cleland's apple snow topping is just one of many ways fruit has been included in trifle. Cooks used what was to hand, and preserved fruit, in the form of jam spread on biscuits or sponges, was followed nearer our own time by bottled or tinned fruit and latterly by fresh berries and tropical fruits.

The heady vapours at the bottom of my grandmother's trifles are the stuff of my earliest memories. She was virtually teetotal and, having no other use for the sherry she bought to make the Hogmanay trifle, poured it with a liberal hand. Was there jelly or fruit in her trifles? Bananas perhaps, but I seem, not surprisingly, to have forgotten.

Then there was school trifle, a dismal business of dry sponge cake encased in bouncy red jelly with a gobbet or two of tinned fruit cocktail, topped with floury custard and that 1950s luxury, a squirt of synthetic cream. Adults who could remember what real cream tasted like did not share our childish liking for the pretend stuff. School trifles, hospital trifles and canteen trifles are not just bad but sad, not so much for their sobriety but for their mean-spirited economy. The trifle formula is simple; the permutations endless. What counts is the quality of the ingredients. The bottom layer needs to be absorbent. It can be of cake, sponge biscuits, ratafias, amaretti, or a mixture of any or all of them. These can all be bought, or made yourself if you fancy baking them, or if you want to use organic ingredients or have hazelnut ratafias instead of the traditional almond ones. Good, but not priceless dessert wines and sherries made with aromatic grapes such as muscat and Pedro Ximinez add more to the final trifle than less characterful blended wines; though fruit juice can take the place of wine in a trifle made without alcohol.

Fruit can be fresh or preserved — anything from strawberry jam and sliced bananas to fresh orange or pear slices, or out-of-season berries. The next big decision is whether to go the whole velvet hog with a custard made from double cream, egg yolks,

sugar and vanilla, or to opt for a carton of fresh custard from the supermarket. Then, to crown it all, there is nothing better than a billowing layer of everlasting syllabub, a sweetly fragrant, winey foam that is even lighter than whipped cream.

Trifle decorations have scarcely changed in three centuries. What were comfits and nonpareils but sugar-candied seeds, flowers and pieces of fruit, the forebears of silver balls and oh-so-retro scarlet glacé cherries flanked by emerald angelica leaves.

A big glass bowl has long been traditional for trifles. But if the whole dessert is unlikely to be eaten at one sitting, there is a lot to be said for making individual trifles, or whim-whams, which are more or less instant trifles, lush with alcohol and a custard-free zone.

pears in perry
& pomegranate syrup

Poach pears in perry or cider for flavour, adding grenadine syrup (made from pomegranates) or cordial for its fabulous colour. Reduce the poaching liquid by at least half to make an intensely flavoured and coloured syrup. Serve the pears in shallow glass dishes, with a spoonful each of the syrup and thick cream or crème fraîche, and a crisp biscuit such as an orange jumble (page 108).

8 firm pears

juice of a lemon

1 litre perry or cider

200ml grenadine syrup or alcoholic cordial

200ml sugar

Using a sharp, swivelling vegetable peeler that takes really thin peelings, carefully peel the pears, leaving the stalks in place. Coring the fruit from the underside by cutting out a cone of flesh with a sharp, pointed knife is an optional refinement. Submerge the peeled fruit in cold water acidulated with the lemon juice to minimize browning.

Chose a wide pan that will hold the pears snugly in single layer. Put the perry or cider, grenadine syrup or cordial and sugar in the pan. Heat gently, stirring until the sugar has dissolved completely. Drain the pears and add to the pan. If they are not completely covered by the liquid, add water. Bring to the boil, lower the heat and simmer very gently until the pears are tender.

Leave the pears to cool in the liquid. When they are completely cold, remove and reserve them. Boil the syrup until it has reduced to about 500ml. Cool the syrup and pour it over the pears. Chill them until needed.

gooseberry
summer pudding

The idea for this pudding comes from a Tudor recipe for buttered gooseberries, which were stewed with sugar and butter, flavoured with rosewater, thickened with eggs and served on snippets of bread. Make the individual puddings in ramekins, dariole or castle pudding moulds, or make one larger pudding in a bowl. Serve with cream that has been lightly sweetened and flavoured with elderflower cordial. Serves six.

at least 12 very thin, crustless slices of day-old white bread

750g green gooseberries

75g unsalted butter

3 tablespoons rosewater

150g sugar, or more to taste

6 leaves gelatine

FOR THE CREAM
300ml double cream, chilled

3 tablespoons elderflower cordial

2 tablespoons caster sugar

Line the moulds or bowl with the crustless bread, cutting the slices to fit neatly without gaps or overlaps – ramekins are easiest to do. Use a pastry cutter to stamp out circles to line the bases – which will become the top of the puddings – and strips to form the walls.

Gently cook the gooseberries with butter and rosewater in a covered pan until soft enough to mash. Pass the fruit through a sieve to remove the seeds and skins. Return the purée to the pan and heat gently, adding enough sugar to sweeten it to your taste.

Soften about six leaves of gelatine in cold water for 5 minutes, then drain and add to the warm purée. Stir until the gelatine has melted completely.

Fill the prepared moulds or bowl with the purée, and leave for 5 minutes to allow the bread to soak up the juices. Top up the level of the purée and cover the moulds at once with clingfilm or foil. Refrigerate until set – allow 2 to 3 hours.

Combine the cream, cordial and sugar in a large chilled bowl and whisk until the mixture holds soft peaks.

To unmould the puddings, dip the moulds briefly in hot water before turning out the puddings on to individual serving plates. Pass round the whipped cream, letting everyone help themselves.

raspberry
& syllabub trifle

The whole point of a trifle is festive, heart-warming extravagance. This syllabub-topped raspberry trifle, with its rich, creamy custard and home-made hazelnut meringue biscuits in the base, is my idea of the perfect trifle. Sweet dessert wines based on highly perfumed muscat grapes and sold in half-bottles are ideal for trifles. Serves eight to ten.

300ml sweet white wine

6 tablespoons Grand Marnier, Cointreau or cognac

1 lemon

100g light brown sugar

150g sponge finger biscuits, bought or home-made, (page 111)

12 hazelnut meringue biscuits (page 111) or amaretti

300g fresh or frozen raspberries

600ml custard made with cream (page 19)

300ml double cream, chilled

sugar-frosted flowers to decorate (page 135)

Put the wine in a jug with the orange liqueur or cognac. Add the juice of the lemon and a few pieces of its thinly pared zest. Stir in the sugar and set the mixture aside, stirring occasionally, until the sugar has dissolved.

Arrange the sponge fingers over the base of a large glass serving bowl. Scatter the hazelnut meringue biscuits and raspberries over them. Remove the lemon zest from the reserved wine mixture and pour half of it over the biscuits and fruit. When the liquid has soaked in, spoon the custard over the fruit in an even layer. Do this while the custard is still hot. Cover and leave the bowl in a cool place for several hours or overnight.

To make the syllabub topping, whisk the reserved wine and liqueur mixture with the chilled cream until the mixture holds soft peaks. Spoon it over the trifle and decorate the top with frosted flowers as you fancy.

strawberry sorbet

Ices get no easier than this smooth, intensely flavoured sorbet. The large amount of sugar creates the silky texture, so don't hesitate to use more lemon juice to balance the taste. Try serving this sweet sorbet, instead of cream, with tart redcurrants, white currants or blackcurrants. Serves six.

500g ripe, fragrant strawberries

freshly squeezed juice of an orange and a lemon

250g caster sugar

Hull the strawberries and purée them with the orange and lemon juice by processing briefly in a blender or food processor and sieving the purée. Stir in the sugar. Let the mixture stand for an hour or two to allow the flavour to develop, stirring it from time to time, until the sugar has dissolved completely.

Freeze the mixture in an ice cream maker until thick and smooth. Serve at once, or turn into a freezer container, cover and store in the freezer.

Alternatively, freeze in a shallow container until frozen but not hard. Turn out into a deep bowl, break up and beat with an electric beater until smooth. Freeze until firm.

Depending on the temperature of the freezer, the sorbet will probably need to be 'ripened' or softened a little before serving. Either transfer it to the refrigerator for 10 to 15 minutes before serving, or microwave on the lowest setting for 2 to 3 minutes.

Serve either on its own, with berries, or as an accompaniment to meringues or vanilla ice cream.

rosemary creams

Sweet rosemary creams are as traditional as country cooking gets, because, of course, herbs pre-date spices as flavourings in the British kitchen. Serves six.

2 sprigs rosemary

300ml double cream

300ml whole milk

50g caster sugar

2 large eggs

sugar-frosted rosemary flowers, or rosemary tufts to decorate

Bruise the rosemary sprigs and put them in a small saucepan with the cream and milk. Heat to just below boiling point, remove from the heat, and set aside until quite cold.

Heat the oven to 140°C/120°C fan oven/gas mark 1. Strain the cream into a bowl, discarding the rosemary, and add the sugar and eggs. Whisk lightly to combine. Strain the mixture again and divide it between six custard cups or small ovenproof dishes. Set them in a roasting tin and pour in boiling water to come halfway up the sides of the small dishes. Bake for about 30 minutes, or until the creams are lightly set.

Chill the creams, and just before serving, sprinkle with crystallized rosemary flowers.

To make sugar-frosted rosemary flowers
In bloom even before the snowdrops, rosemary flowers range in colour from white and pink through to palest lavender and a deep, true blue. Pick newly opened blooms on a dry day and treat them immediately. When sugared and dried, they will keep for a year or more.

Use a fork to break up an egg white in a saucer, frothing it lightly. Half-fill another saucer with sugar and lay a sheet of writing or drawing paper on a dish or tray. Using a small brush, such as a watercolour brush, paint a flower lightly with egg white. Drop it into the sugar and sprinkle more sugar over it. Shake off any excess sugar and transfer the flower to the paper. Painting the first few tiny blooms feels absurdly fiddly, but expertise comes quickly.

Paint and sugar the remaining flowers the same way. Dry them in the oven, set at the lowest possible temperature, for up to 12 hours if they can stay there without taking colour, or leave them in a warm airing cupboard for several days. To preserve the colour and perfume of the flowers, store them out of the light in an airtight container.

Violet and primrose blooms can be sugar-frosted using the same method.

soft fruit
& orange sabayon

Grill soft fruit under a froth of sabayon sauce to create a fast and wickedly moreish pudding. Serves four.

400g mixed soft fruit

6 egg yolks

100g caster sugar

150ml freshly squeezed orange juice

2 tablespoons raspberry or orange liqueur

Divide the fruit between four shallow, heatproof dishes and heat up the grill.

Whisk the egg yolks and sugar in a heatproof bowl until pale, then set the bowl over a pan of simmering water. Whisking constantly, gradually add the orange juice until the mixture is thick enough to leave a ribbon trail from the whisk. Whisk in the liqueur.

Pour the sabayon over the fruit and grill the dishes until the surface is lightly caramelized. Serve at once.

whim-wham

Easy enough to make on a whim, and certainly packing a wham, whim-whams are as instant as trifles get. Make in one large, traditional, cut-glass trifle bowl, or in individual goblets. The sponge finger biscuits retain a little of their crispness when a whim-wham is a last-minute creation. Serves six.

25g butter

100g flaked almonds

1 tablespoon caster sugar

120g sponge finger biscuits, bought or home-made (page 111)

100ml fresh orange juice or tangerine juice

120ml fine sweet sherry

120ml brandy

450ml double cream or whipping cream

In a heavy frying pan, fry the almonds in the butter until they are golden. Sprinkle them with the sugar and shake the pan on a low heat until the sugar melts. Turn the almonds on to a lightly greased surface and spread them out to cool.

An hour or two before serving the whim-whams, break the sponge fingers into six individual glasses or dishes or into one large serving dish. Combine the orange juice, sherry and brandy and pour the mixture over the biscuits.

When the sponge fingers have absorbed most of the liquid, whisk the cream until it holds soft peaks and spoon it over the biscuits. Sprinkle the caramelized almonds over the top and serve.

fresh lemonade

Keep a jug of fresh lemon cordial in the refrigerator to make real lemonade at a moment's notice. Makes 1 litre.

6 juicy lemons

400g sugar

Squeeze the juice from the lemons and strain it into a jug. Mix with the sugar and stir to dissolve. Chill until needed.

To serve, pour a generous measure of lemon syrup into a tumbler and top up with still or carbonated iced water.

index

A

almond pastry 105
anchovies: lamb with rosemary,
    garlic & anchovy 48
animal welfare 33

B

bacon & egg salad 15
baking 96–113
biscuits, hazelnut meringue 111
biscuits, oatmeal 108
biscuits, orange jumbles 108
biscuits, sponge finger 111–12
bread 97–9
bread, brown 100
breadmakers 98
butter 99
    cake, honey & orange drizzle 109
    pastry, almond 105
    pastry, sweet 104
    pizza 103
    shortbread, butterscotch 112
    strudels, strawberry 106
    yeast 98
basil & ricotta ravioli 23
basmati rice: orange pilau 73
beans
    broad bean omelette 18
    minestrone 63
    salmon with beans & fennel 83
    & truffle soup 60
beef
    boiled with dumplings 38
    salt brisket 37
biscuits
    hazelnut meringue 111
    oatmeal 108
    orange jumbles 108
    sponge finger 111–12
black cabbage: minestrone 63
borlotti beans: minestrone 63
boudoir biscuits 111
bread 97–9
brown 100
breadmakers 98
brisket
    boiled with dumplings 38
    salt 37

broad bean omelette with mint &
    ricotta 18
burnt honey & orange drizzle cake
    109
butter 9–10
    baking with 99
    clarified 28
    herb 25
butternut squash: roasted with
    pancetta & pasta 74
butterscotch shortbread 112

C

cake: honey & orange drizzle 109
cannellini beans
    minestrone 63
    & truffle soup 60
capers: halibut with sage butter &
    95
caviar: creamed eggs 12
cheese pudding 17
chestnuts: mushroom, leek &
    chestnut jalousies 58
chicken 32
    with rosemary & pine nuts 39
chives: baked eggs 14
chowder: prawn 86
clarified butter 28
Cleland, Elizabeth 128
cod 79
cooking, modern 6–7
cordial: lemon 138
Country Living Magazine 7
courgettes: stuffed 70
couscous: vegetables 71
crab 79
    fresh 80
    omelette 82
    potted 28
crab apples: & rowanberry jelly 121
cream
    baked eggs 14
custard 19
    rosemary creams 135
    trifle, raspberry 132
    whim-wham 138
curd
    Seville orange 125

    strawberry 125
custards 19

D

dairy 8–29
    bacon & egg salad 15
    butter, clarified 28
    butter, flavoured 25
    cheese pudding 17
    crab, potted 28
    egg pasta 20
    eggs, baked with cream &
        chives 14
    eggs, creamed with caviar 12
    hollandaise sauce 26
    mayonnaise 27
    omelette, broad bean 18
    pastry cream 19
    ravioli, basil & ricotta 23
    ravioli, pumpkin 22
desserts 126–39
    pears in perry 130
    rosemary creams 135
    sabayon, fruit & orange 137
    sorbet, strawberry 134
    summer pudding, gooseberry 131
    trifle 127–9
    trifle, raspberry & syllabub 132
    whim-wham 138
duck
    confit of duck legs 34
    salt 37
dumplings: boiled beef & 38

E

eggs 10–11
    baked with cream & chives 14
    cheese pudding 17
    creamed with caviar 12
    custard 19
    hollandaise sauce 26
    mayonnaise 27
    omelette, broad bean with mint
        and ricotta 18
    omelette, crab 82
    pasta, fresh 20
    pastry cream 19
    salad, bacon & egg 15

emulsion sauces 11

F
farmers' markets 9, 11, 31, 32

fennel: salmon with beans & 83
fish 76–95
  buying 78–9
  chowder, prawn 86
  crab, fresh 80
  crab, omelette 82
  halibut, roast 95
  herring, soused 94
  mackerel pâté 87
  mussels, stuffed 88
  oily 78
  organic 78, 79
  salmon, pickled 90
  salmon, roast 83
  salmon, tartare of fresh &
    smoked 91
  scampi à la meunière 85–6
  shrimp fritters 93
fruit & orange sabayon 137

G
game 33
  pie 42–4
garlic: lamb with rosemary, garlic
  & anchovy 48
gin: pickled salmon 90
Glasse, Hannah 128
gooseberry summer pudding 131
gravadlax 90

H
halibut 79
  roast with sage butter & capers 95
harissa: couscous & vegetables 71
hazelnut meringue biscuits 111
herb butter 25
herring 79
  soused 94
hollandaise sauce 26
honey & orange drizzle cake 109

I
ingredients 6

J
jars 117
Jekyll, Agnes 108
juniper: pickled salmon 90

K
kidneys: mushroom & kidney pies 50

L
Lady Jekyll's orange jumbles 108
lamb
  roast leg with rosemary, garlic &
    anchovy 48
  sauté of lamb with lemon 49
leeks
  gratin 65
  jalousies 58
lemonade 138
lemons
  lamb 49
  lemonade 138
  potatoes, baked 67
lentils
  cakes, potato 68
  soup 62

M
mackerel: pâté 87
Marine Conservation Society 79
marmalade 116
  Scotch 124
mayonnaise 27
meat 30–53
  beef, boiled with dumplings 38
  brisket, salt 37
  chicken, with rosemary & pine
    nuts 39
  cured 33
  duck, confit of duck legs 34
  duck, salt 37
  fat in 32
  lamb, roast leg of 48
  lamb, sautéed 49
  locally produced 31
  mushroom & kidney pies 50
  organic 32
  partridge, pot roast 45
  partridge pudding 40–1
  pork, roast 53
  quality 31–3
  venison pasty 42–4
  venison ragout 47
milk
  cheese pudding 17
  pastry cream 19
  pork, roast 53
minestrone 63
mint: broad bean omelette with

ricotta 18
modern cooking 6–7
mushroom & kidney pies 50
mushroom, leek & chestnut
  jalousies 58
mussels: stuffed 88

O
oatmeal biscuits 108
oily fish 78
omelette: broad bean with mint &
  ricotta 18
onions: sweet & sour (caramelised)
  75
oranges
  biscuits, orange jumbles 108
  cake, honey & orange drizzle 109
  curd, Seville orange 125
  Scotch marmalade 124
  pilau 73
  sabayon, fruit & orange 137
organic fish 78, 79
organic meat 32
organic vegetables 56

P
pancetta: butternut squash 74
parmesan: pumpkin ravioli 22
partridge
  pot roast 45
  pudding 40–1
pasta
  butternut squash, roasted 74
  fresh egg 20
  ravioli, basil & ricotta ravioli 23
  ravioli, pumpkin 22
  venison ragout 47
pastry
  almond 105
  sweet 104
pastry cream 19
pears in perry & pomegranate
  syrup 130
pies
  mushroom & kidney 50
  mushroom, leek & chestnut
    jalousies 58
  venison pasty 42–4
pine nuts: chicken with rosemary &
  39
pistou: soupe au 59
pizza: thin 103
pork 32

roasted in milk 53
potatoes
    baked, festive 66
    baked, lemon 67
    cakes, lentil 68
    gratin, leek 65
potted crab 28
prawns
    chowder 86
    fritters 93
preserves 114–25
    jars 117
    marmalade 116
    orange curd 125
    raspberry jelly 120
    rhubarb & vanilla jam 123
    rowanberry & crab apple jelly
        121
    Scotch marmalade 124
    strawberry curd 125
    strawberry & redcurrant jelly 118
    sugar 117
puddings *see* desserts
pumpkin ravioli with sage &
    parmesan 22

R
Rare Breeds Survival Trust 31
raspberries
    jelly 120
    trifle 132
ravioli
    basil & ricotta 23
    pumpkin 22
redcurrants: & strawberry jelly 118
rhubarb & vanilla jam 123
rice: orange pilau 73
ricotta
    omelette, broad bean 18
    ravioli, basil & ricotta 23
rosemary
    chicken with rosemary & pine
        nuts 39
    lamb with rosemary, garlic &
        anchovy 48
rosemary creams 135
rowanberry & crab apple jelly 121

S
sabayon: fruit & orange 137
sage
    halibut with sage butter 95
    ravioli, pumpkin 22

salads 55
    bacon & egg 15
salmon
    farmed 78
    organic 78
    pickled 90
    roast with beans & fennel 83
    tartare of fresh & smoked 91
    wild 78
salt brisket 37
salt duck 37
salting 33
sauces
    emulsion 11
    hollandaise 26
    mayonnaise 27
scampi à la meunière 85–6
Scotch marmalade 124
Seville oranges
    curd 125
    marmalade 124
shellfish: farmed 79
shortbread: butterscotch 112
shrimp fritters 93
sorbet: strawberry 134
soups
    bean & truffle 60
    minestrone 63
    prawn chowder 86
    soupe au pistou 59
    tarka dhal 62
sponge finger biscuits 111–12
stock: vegetable 60
strawberries
    curd 125
    and redcurrant jelly 118
    sorbet 134
    strudels 106
strudel: strawberry 106
suet pudding: partridge 40–1
sugar 117
summer pudding: gooseberries 131
supermarkets 32
sweet pastry 104

T
tarka dhal soup 62
thyme
    leek gratin 65
    onions, sweet & sour 75
trifles 127–9
    raspberry & syllabub 132
    whim-wham 138

turbot 79

V
vanilla
    custard 19
    pastry cream 19
    rhubarb jam 123
vegetables 54–75
    butternut squash, roasted 74
    cooking 56–7
    courgettes, stuffed 70
    couscous & 71
    fresh 55–6
    leek, thyme & potato gratin 65
    lentil & potato cakes 68
    mushroom, leek & chestnut
        jalousies 58
    onions with thyme 75
    organic 56
    pests 56
    pilau, orange 73
    potatoes, festive baked 66
    potatoes, lemon baked 67
    range of 55
    salads 55
    soupe, au pistou 59
    soup, bean & truffle 60
    soup, minestrone 63
    soup, tarka dhal 62
    stock 60
venison
    pasty 42–4
    ragout with pasta 47

W
whim-wham 138
white bean & truffle soup 60

Y
yeast 98

useful addresses

Marine Conservation Society's website at www.fishonline.org builds on the information contained in its Good Fish Guide with definitive advice for over 125 fish species. A rating of 1 to 5 is given for each fish stock or species dependent on its status, sustainability and fisheries impact.

All you need to know about organic issues plus suppliers from **The Soil Association**. www.soilassociation.org

All you need to know about rare breed animals, plus suppliers of livestock and produce from

The Rare Breeds Survivial Trust www.rbst.org.uk

Organically reared geese and ducks by mail order from **Exmoor Organic** www.exmoor-organic.co.uk

Organically reared chickens by mail order from **Sheepdrove Farm** in Berkshire www.sheepdrove.co.uk

Barley couscous and rose harissa, a fiery seasoning paste moderated with rose petals, are made by **belazu**. For stockists www.belazu.com

Dorset Pastry makes a range of real butter pastry, including puff. For mail order and stockists www.dorsetpastry.com

Saltpetre for can be bought by mail order from **Natural Casing Company** telephone 01252 850454